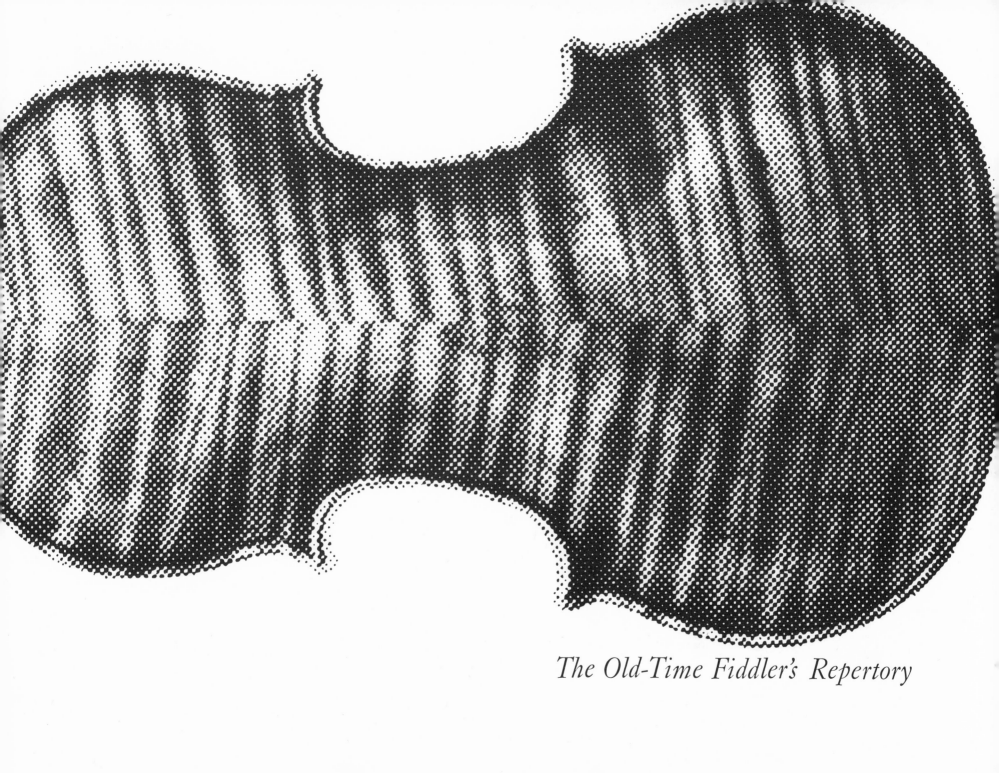

The Old-Time Fiddler's Repertory

University of Missouri Press · *1973*

The Old-Time Fiddler's Repertory

245 Traditional Tunes

Compiled and edited by R. P. Christeson

Copyright © 1973 by The Curators of the University of Missouri

University of Missouri Press, Columbia, Missouri 65201

Library of Congress Catalog Number 73–80036   ISBN 0–8262–0151–2

Printed and bound in the United States of America   All rights reserved

Dedication

To all old-time fiddlers in the past who brought fun and pleasure

into the lives of their friends and neighbors, and to the many fiddlers

who generously and patiently gave of their time and efforts to make this

collection possible, this publication is respectfully dedicated.

Acknowledgments

A list of the people who contributed toward this publication either by their encouragement or by their participation, limited or extensive, would be quite lengthy and difficult to compile.

The completion of this publication, however, would have been considerably delayed, if not postponed indefinitely, without the valuable help of friends with musical skill.

I am grateful to Mrs. H. L. (Billie) Anderton of Arlington, Virginia, for her generous assistance to me in the rudimentary techniques of transferring fiddle tunes to the printed page.

I owe special appreciation to Miss Kathy Goldman of Washington, D.C., for her editorial suggestions in the manuscript and for testing the piano scores at the keyboard.

Also, my deepest gratitude to Mrs. Jan Lloyd of Sturgeon, Missouri, for painstakingly reviewing the completed musical portions, measure by measure, for details such as poorly drawn note heads, missing repeat marks, key signature omissions, and other related items in the technique of music notation.

Finally, my greatest thanks are due to my wife, Joan, who patiently allowed a room in the house to remain cluttered with musical materials for many months.

R. P. C.
Auxvasse, Missouri
May, 1973

References

The books in the following list contain information that interested me, as I believe it will interest others who want to know more about fiddle tunes. Some of them are mentioned in the notes to the tunes.

Adams, E. F. *Old-Time Fiddlers Favorite Barn Dance Tunes*. St. Louis, 1927.

Allan's Ballroom Companion.

Bayard, Samuel P. *Hill Country Tunes*. University of Pennsylvania Press, Harrisburg, 1944.

Cole, M. M., and Company. *1000 Fiddle Tunes*. Chicago, 1940.

Ford, Henry. *The Dearborn Independent*. Dearborn, Mich., 1926.

Ford, Ira. *Traditional Music of America*. E. P. Dutton Company, New York, 1940.

Howe, Elias A. *Diamond School for the Violin*. Boston, n.d.

———. *Musician's Omnibus Complete*. Boston, n.d.

———. *Musician's Omnibus Complete Improved Edition*. Boston, 1864.

———. *Ryan's Jigs and Reels*. Boston, 1883.

Jarman, Harry E. *Old-Time Fiddlin' Tunes*. Toronto, 1938.

Kerr, J. S. *Kerr's Collection of Reels, Strathspeys, Highland Schottisches, Country Dances, Jigs, Hornpipes, Flirtations, etc*. Glasgow, n.d.

Knauff, G. P. *Virginia Reels*. George Willig, Baltimore, [184–].

Morris, Dr. W. H. *Old-Time Violin Melodies*. St. Joseph, Mo., 1927.

Roche, F. *Collection of Irish Airs, Marches & Dance Tunes*. Dublin, 1911.

Routh, Viola (Mom). *Pioneer Western Folk Tunes*. Phoenix, Ariz., 1948.

Thede, Marion. *The Fiddle Book*. Oak Publications, New York, 1968.

White-Smith Publishing Co. *White's Unique Collection of Jigs, Reels, etc. for the Violin*. Boston, 1896.

Contents

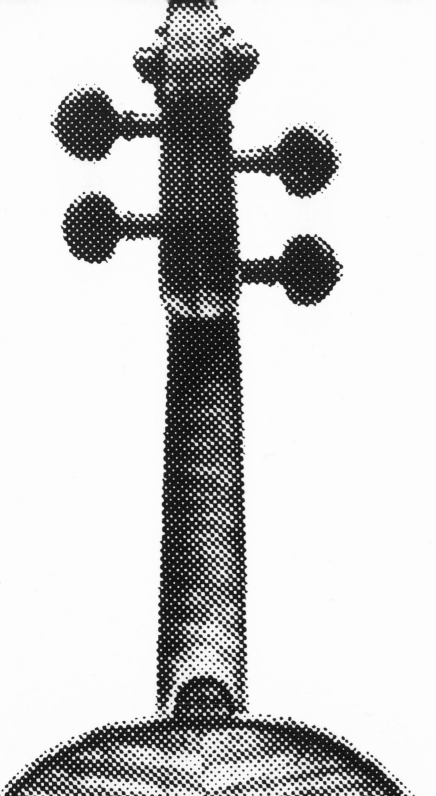

Introduction

    E. F. Adam, in his fine book of 1931, *Old-Time Fiddlers Favorite Barn Dance Tunes,* wrote that America was indebted to its old-time fiddlers for keeping alive an interest in the violin which encouraged people to undertake formal violin study.

    I would add another contribution made by the fiddler and his music which has received little recognition. The routine of living for many people during the growth of this country was not without dreariness and hardships. Anything that would offer some enjoyment amid unpleasant conditions was highly desirable. It also had to be within their means. The gathering of neighbors for an old-time square dance met both of these criteria. Here, to the peppy breakdowns, reels, hornpipes, quadrilles, jigs, etc., provided by the fiddler, they could indulge in some fun—defined here as being generated by the individual participant; in contrast, entertainment is provided by others. This is how many people would lay aside their troubles and rekindle their energies for the difficulties ahead. In addition to dances, there were musical gatherings where the hearing and playing of these old tunes would help dissolve fatigue and promote relaxation. Fiddle music made a definite contribution toward the amelioration of a harsh and difficult existence and fostered neighborliness among many people.

    I believe old-time tunes and country-style square dancing still merit inclusion in the sociocultural fabric of the American people.

    Reasons other than this belief, however, led me toward collecting the old-time fiddle music gathered in this publication. By way of background for my interest: I was born at a point in time (1911) and in space (Pulaski County, Missouri) in which old-time fiddling and square dancing flourished and were integral components of the mores of the people. Fiddlers would frequently congregate in town at night or on Saturday for the fun of playing, and they always drew an audience. Schoolboys carried harmonicas or jew's-harps for playing at recess. The ratio of good jig dancers, both male and female, to total population in Pulaski County was high. Square dances were numerous and well attended, with the calling shared by many, as each set had its own caller. Square dancing did not give way to the play party, although dancing was condemned by some preachers who referred to the fiddle as the "Devil's instrument." It might be added that there were no folk singers in the modern image in this locality, even though many individuals had a few songs they could sing. I had to live an additional thirty years before I saw my first hirsute folk singer.

There was an eighteen-year dormancy in my involvement with fiddle music, extending from 1928, when I played in a fiddler's contest in my home town as a college freshman, to 1946, when I resumed going to square dances. By 1946 I was a resident of southern New Mexico, where old-time fiddling and old-style square dances still prevailed.

In New Mexico I noticed that many of the tunes I had heard at dances in Missouri in the 1920s were not being played in the Southwest. My efforts to help a local fiddler learn additional tunes were made difficult by the long lapse in my fiddling. My difficulties prompted me to undertake a rather fruitless effort: an attempt to get a supply of old-time fiddle tunes by mail order. I was unaware, in the beginning, that so few books on the subject had been published and were so difficult to locate. I was surprised at the high proportion of people in the music trade who seemed to have a near-zero awareness of the existence of old fiddle music. On rare occasions a dealer would suggest a book of jigs and reels, if he had one in stock. The frustrations in trying to find on the market and purchase a book of old-time fiddle tunes in the mid-1940s were, it turned out, many and very discouraging.

I now see this particular effort in a different perspective. My expecting a book of old-time fiddle tunes to be commercially available was not greatly different than expecting to find a selection of books for beginners in bicycle riding. I had simply not recognized fiddling as a self-taught folk art which was largely maintained by custom and propagated by imitation.

In a related effort, I wrote the chairmen of the music departments at several land-grant colleges, inquiring whether any students or staff members had ever sought out any old-time fiddlers and had written down their tunes for research or other purposes. It was soon apparent from the negative replies that this quest was to be barren.

I then tried another source: the recording industry. From dealers and collectors I accumulated a substantial number of 78-rpm fiddle records. Several of these recordings were quite good, but it is my opinion that posterity would have been little deprived if the remainder had never been issued. It is lamentable that the recording companies did not seek out fiddlers like Matt Brown

of Texas, Bob Walters of Nebraska, or Bill Caton, Dallas Stamper, Jim Gilpin, and Bill Driver of Missouri.

These unproductive efforts to obtain the desired music by mail or on records led me to purchase a wire recorder to do my own collecting. Bill Driver, then living in Cole County, Missouri, had replied to an earlier letter that he would be ready to play. I took the recorder along during my annual vacation, and a recording session on July 7, 1948, was the first of many in the years to follow.

Gathering fiddle music proved to be a fascinating endeavor. In the ensuing years, I ultimately recorded individual fiddlers in eight states and contests in four states, in addition to the 1950 Annual Texas Fiddlers Convention at Athens, Texas, which I recorded in its entirety.

In 1949, I was transferred from New Mexico to Nebraska, from there to Indiana in 1956, and to Washington, D.C., in 1961; after the last transfer I did very little recording.

Over the years, I have seldom made any trip, business or pleasure, without taking the recorder. My goal was always to seek out the best fiddlers, more particularly those experienced in playing for dances, and to record in depth through several sessions. The close of each recording session left me wondering whether I had been probing the tip of a musical iceberg. Was I delving into a still existing musical heritage of huge dimensions or into one greatly shrunken by the disappearance of large portions which could never be salvaged?

In my recording experiences I met many fine gentlemen who, except for one jealous individual in Texas, were most cooperative. On numerous occasions the fiddler was not playing with a regular group, and I served as his accompanist. Few of the fiddlers had ever been approached about recording or preserving their tunes. I also noticed that few of them had sons or daughters who played or were going to become fiddlers and carry on the family tradition.

Since 1961, each succeeding obituary for another of the fiddlers who once played for me also meant that some good tunes had likely gone to the cemetery. I began to question why people in the future should not be allowed to play, hear, or dance to the music of the Bill Drivers or the Bob Walterses. Hence, the decision to transcribe this collection from the wire recordings. I hope this book, the result of that decision, will give some recognition to the individual fiddlers who have kept these tunes alive during the years and will provide enjoyment for people in the future. The existing literature on old-time fiddling will also be enlarged.

This book is not offered as a complete compilation of the old tunes. It is comprised principally of the fiddle music certain fiddlers recorded in certain areas at a certain time. A few tunes from my own memory are included, although I cannot recall their sources.

The majority of tunes in this book are dance tunes of one class or another. They are not "Western" square-dance tunes in the modern sense, even though several of them were regularly played at square dances in New Mexico, West Texas, Colorado, and Arizona during the late 1940s. In New Mexico where I lived, the square dancers shared the rent on a building, hired live music when not making their own, did all of their own calling, and broke in new dancers. It was about 1948 when "Western" square dancing appeared, bringing with it the paid singing-caller with his record player, the formal practice lessons, the literature, and the fancy costumes. Beginning at that time, the term "square dancing" might refer either to the original do-it-for-fun hoedown or to a new form of catered entertainment.

Considerable material is excluded from this book. The version I recorded for some tunes was not significantly different from that already published, and I omitted them. "Soldier's Joy" is an example. I also withheld several songs which some fiddlers play, minus their lyrics, as tunes. "Casey Jones" is in this category. Several tunes were eliminated at the recording sessions or later because the tune was not amenable to orthodox accompaniment, due to irregular metering. "Fire on the Mountain" is a case in point, as it extends beyond the finish of standard phrasing. I have left out the neotraditional tunes, such as "Orange Blossom Special," and have presented no tunes that require cross-tuning. Most discord playing I have heard and seen has been of the novelty variety and musically unequal to a well-played breakdown in the standard tuning for square dances.

Some tunes of lesser quality are presented in this collection, since they form a part of the spectrum and apparently have not been documented previously. Although I have excluded numerous hornpipes, jigs, and reels that have continued with minimum changes in title or detail since the Civil War or before and are still available in printed form, I have included some reels and hornpipes that have undergone certain evolutionary modifications in the past hundred years.

Some tunes published as early as the Civil War are still alive, but they have acquired different titles. The more obvious cases are mentioned in the notes. I was not fully aware until compiling this book how often the names of tunes were either unknown or overlooked by the fiddler or by myself. The titles are those given by the fiddlers, and I have not changed any. No particular effort has been made to provide extensive references or other analytical detail on individual tunes such as was so ably done by Professor Samuel P. Bayard in his scholarly work, *Hill Country Tunes*. This book is not a research project, and the relationship of its individual tunes to antecedent tunes, published or unpublished, is left to future researchers. The part for piano or parlor organ is given for one breakdown in each key. There is also one example in each of the other groups, Quadrilles, Pieces, and Waltzes. An informative discussion on piano accompaniment for fiddle tunes is given in Ira Ford's *Traditional Music of America*. This old-time style of accompaniment traditionally employs the subdominant chord in the 6th measure for the standard breakdown, which has 8 measures per part. Except among aging accompanists, this old system is heard less and less today.

A metronome speed is given above each tune with piano accompaniment, and for several tunes in the Pieces category. While these suggested tempos are by no means rigid, they are realistic and should have equal validity for fiddlers today as they did for fiddlers earlier. Experienced dance fiddlers in the past could judge the optimum tempo simply by observing the dancers while playing.

A few of the basic accompaniments employed years ago by the second fiddle are included. One of the characteristic old-time Missouri fiddle bands consisted of first fiddle, second fiddle, and piano or parlor organ. The second fiddle and its technique are rarely used today, and this art may be nearing extinction. The second-fiddle accompaniments for breakdowns are given immediately after the tunes. I have had limited formal musical training and regret the technical inability to indicate the various subtleties and techniques employed by some of the old-timers in their bowing and fingering. The articulation of individual tunes, however, cannot be standardized anyway, as the old-time fiddler will typically adopt his own interpretation of individual numbers.

This book is presented in the hope that succeeding generations will keep these tunes alive.

The Fiddlers

The search for fiddle music in different sections of the country led to many lasting friendships. People with mutual interests in old-time fiddling will often establish a rapport rather quickly. What follows is from my recollections of those earlier fiddlers.

The Bell Family, originally from Howell County, Missouri, was en route to California from Oklahoma at the time they stopped in New Mexico and began playing for square dances in the late 1940s. The father played on a high-grade violin of German origin and was assisted by a son and daughter. They had an adequate group of tunes for square dances but specialized in music for entertainments and parties.

The Black Brothers of Hatch, Dona Ana County, New Mexico, played for local square dances. Their orchestra was composed of family members and was generally available unless the travel requirements conflicted with their regular occupation of operating a lumber yard. I did not record them directly, so I have relied on memory for their music in this book.

Jesse Cain was a distant cousin of mine in Dixon, Pulaski County, Missouri. I was in grade school when Jesse was doing most of his playing in the 1920s, and I regret my inability to recall more of Jesse's tunes, including a particularly fine waltz on the lower register.

Bill Caton (fiddle) and Ola Gathright (guitar) comprised a widely known duo of colored musicians in Callaway County, Missouri, who often played over WOS at Jefferson City. I can recall listening to them in the late 1920s by joining a group in front of the Leader Store. This grocery on the town's main street had the only radio in town with a loud speaker (a battery-operated Atwater-Kent). In 1952 I located Ola Gathright, then living near a small town on the river below Jefferson City and, through him, located Bill Caton's son John in Jefferson City. John recorded several numbers for me, but he did not play the fiddle regularly and could recall only a portion of his dad's tunes. He described one evening at home when Bill got out the fiddle and asked John's mother to keep a record of the tunes, which she did by making tally marks on the wall with a nail. John said his dad played 165 tunes before midnight. Neighboring fiddlers who were closely associated with Bill Caton were Vee Latty and Seth Bradley, both now deceased, and it is not now possible to re-

assemble Bill Caton's repertory. In an interview on tape August 12, 1957, Uncle Bob Walters mentioned he had listened to them over WOS and described their music as "tops."

Ardell Christopher of El Paso, Texas, played for many square dances in the El Paso–southern New Mexico area in the late 1940s. He was stationed at a remote Air Force installation in New Mexico during World War II and learned many fiddle tunes from a retired farmer nearby. Ardell won the California state fiddling championship one year in the early 1950s. He was transferred to headquarters of the Strategic Air Command at Omaha, Nebraska, where he recorded on several occasions while I was living in Lincoln.

Junior Daugherty of Hot Springs, Sierra County, New Mexico, entered a fiddlers contest at El Paso, Texas, in May 1949. His cousin played the guitar, and both were using instruments made by their grandfather. They recorded several pieces for me during their warm-up prior to the contest.

Frame Davis of Des Moines, Iowa, was a railroad engineer and deeply interested in old-time fiddling. He regularly hosted a large get-together of musicians at his home each summer. He lamented the fact that he was not near any good fiddlers during his earlier years while learning to play.

Fred Doxstadter was a violin repairman in Lincoln, Nebraska, who loved old fiddle music and hated popular music with equal passion. He constantly referred to people who played modern music as "jazz pimps." He was born in New York State but spent his childhood in South Dakota, where his parents had taken a homestead. "Doc" could recall many details of the 1888 blizzard. He played a considerable number of tunes, but an early injury to his left hand inhibited his skill.

William A. (Bill) Driver was one of two famed colored fiddlers in Missouri. He was born at Eldridge in Laclede County and later moved to Iberia in Miller County, where he spent most of his playing career. He was gifted with talent, had a keen ear, steady time, and played vigorously. My first contact with Bill's music was at one of the annual summer encampments at Iberia, Missouri, in the late 1920s. This was a six-day picnic and celebration that was first organized to honor Civil War veterans. Bill played for the outdoor dance floor at the encampment and had a large repertory of breakdowns suitable for square dances. This was one of the sections of Missouri where both men and women would jig dance throughout the figures. This required steady, peppy fiddle music, which Bill could provide in abundance. He won many local contests but was never sponsored for any of the state contests. On one occasion, local townspeople arranged for him to play a program over WOS at Jefferson City. This one appearance brought mail from listeners in several states and Canada. (WOS has long since discontinued broadcasting live fiddle music.) Bill represented the best example I encountered of a repertory strictly indigenous to a local area. In contrast to fiddlers in the Boone County area, for example, Bill's repertory was largely undiluted with hornpipes, jigs, or reels, which obviously came from the phonograph, or from the printed page shipped in by mail, or from an itinerant fiddler.

I had numerous recording sessions, beginning in the summer of 1948, at which time Bill was living in a rural section of Cole County in a house without electricity. It was necessary to go elsewhere in order to operate the wire recorder, and sessions were often held at the homes of various cooperative neighbors and acquaintances. Bill moved to Jefferson City about 1952. The last recording session was at his daughter's home one evening, with a large audience of listeners in the front yard. Bill was in his late sixties and past his fiddling prime when the recordings were made. It was necessary to write a considerable number of Bill's tunes from memory, as most of my collection of wires was stolen from its storage place in Missouri in 1966.

Tony Gilmore, a resident of Jefferson City, Missouri, was a railroad conductor by vocation and a fiddler by avocation. Tony had a large repertory and enjoyed playing in contests. He once swapped runs on the railroad with another conductor in order to be near Fort Smith, Arkansas, when a big contest was to be held. As a youth he lived in Camden County, Missouri, where he learned to jig dance. Tony was the last fiddler I ever saw who could actually dance a jig and play the fiddle simultaneously. Tony recorded on several occasions, and I always looked forward to annual vacations with a side trip to Tony's for a prolonged session of old-time fiddling.

Jack Harris of Jefferson, Harrison County, Texas, attended the Texas Fiddlers Convention at Athens in 1950. He recorded several tunes at his home following the convention; he was a cordial host in addition to being a good player. Harris operated a hardware store and his fiddling was a hobby. He followed the style and moderate tempo most often heard in East Texas.

Burnis Harrison of rural Miller County, Missouri, was a farmer living in the general vicinity of Dallas Stamper and Bill Driver. Burnis could play a few of the Dallas Stamper tunes and I concentrated on these tunes at a recording session in July, 1950.

The Heltons. Anyone by the name of Helton and living in the general area of Dixon, Missouri, in the 1920s was a fiddler. Among the entire clan I was best acquainted with Waldo and Allen, two brothers who lived on a small farm northwest of town. Waldo played lead fiddle with a style that made listeners eager to dance. Allen played second fiddle, an art that has now practically disappeared. Allen once ventured he was the only fiddler who ever learned to play while running. Waldo, being older, was the first to own a fiddle. Allen would borrow it without permission and continue to play while being chased by Waldo as he tried to retrieve the fiddle. They played for the outdoor square dance at each Fourth of July picnic in the city park in Dixon, Missouri. George Helton, who lives in Maries County, Missouri, is a relative of Waldo and Allen and plays quite a few of the old tunes of the area. He plays vigorously, and he made some recordings for me in 1952. Ike Helton, also living in Maries County, is one of the few remaining fiddling Heltons. He is the son of Arch Helton, who won his share of fiddling contests in and around Dixon, Missouri.

Zeke Holdren of Lincoln, Nebraska, was versatile on the violin, piano, and guitar. He was not an old-time fiddler in a strict sense, but could play several tunes acceptably. He learned a few tunes from Sam Stauffer, a transplanted Kentuckian who moved to Lincoln prior to 1900. According to Zeke, hiring Sam to play for a dance would involve advancing Sam enough money to get his fiddle out of pawn. Sam is credited with shooting the horse out from under the Lincoln chief of police as he was riding toward Sam's house (in what is now University Place) with an arrest warrant.

Casey Jones of Livingston County, Missouri, was hired by the Henry Fields Seed Company of Shenandoah, Iowa, in the late 1920s, at which time Casey began playing over the Fields's radio stations at Shenandoah and at Norfolk, Nebraska. Casey later moved to Chillicothe, Iowa, and attended the Frame Davis get-togethers in the early 1950s.

Cyril Kines of Fauquier County, Virginia, is an avid old-time fiddler in an area where old-time square dances are nonexistent. He uses a bowing accent on a few of his tunes that is difficult to analyze or describe, but it is most intriguing and conjures up the impression of a distinctive fiddling technique that might have been common in eastern Virginia at some time in the past.

Vee Latty lived west of Fulton, Callaway County, and was Missouri state champion in 1928. He had the best wrist action with his bow of any country fiddler I ever met. Mr. Latty was a well-known radio fiddler and appeared frequently on WOS, Jefferson City, in the late 1920s, when Friday nights were devoted to fiddling. He also played for Henry Fields over KFNF at Shenandoah, Iowa. Mr. Latty claimed he was the first performer on radio to include a hymn tune on each program.

"Uncle" Jimmy Lewis was a devotee of old-time fiddling who ran a music store in Richland, Pulaski County, Missouri. I had only limited exposure to Uncle Jimmy's playing but recall that customers would frequently request him to play "Money Musk."

Charlie Lutz of York County, Pennsylvania, is an elderly fiddler who last attended the annual Pennsylvania Old Fiddlers Reunion in 1965. It was near the close of the 1965 reunion when Pete Krause, a guitarist, asked Charlie to play a tune "for old times' sake." Charlie played "Sticks and Stones." Pete is an old-time guitarist who wears finger picks and thus is able to play 6/8 tempo properly. This tune was so unusual that I made a special trip to Pennsylvania in 1966 to see whether it could be salvaged. I finally located Mr. Lutz, who graciously arose from his sickbed to record "Sticks and Stones" for me.

Thomas Michaels of Sweetwater, Texas, came to El Paso to play in a fiddlers contest in May, 1949. He played one of the best tunes I ever heard. He was sorely handicapped by an inept guitar player who had been provided by contest officials for the out-of-town fiddlers who did not bring a second. I have no background information on Mr. Michaels who, at that time, was rather elderly.

Paul (Blackie) Morgan is unique, since he is a native of Washington, D.C., with a wide repertory of old-time fiddle tunes. He has indicated his father was a fiddler by hobby. Blackie played many square dances in the Washington, D.C., area in the 1940s for Ralph Case, a well-known caller originally from North Carolina.

George Morris, who was living in St. Louis in the 1950s, was originally from Columbia, Boone County, Missouri, where he was widely known as "the Fiddling Sheriff." George was a very skillful fiddler but did not gain prominence until after beginning a term in the Missouri State Penitentiary for a violation of a bench parole in the 1920s and there came to the attention of the governor who enjoyed good fiddling. George became a trusty, served as chauffeur for the governor, and achieved wide publicity playing over WOS radio in Jefferson City, where the prison is located. He was a member of the old Blue Goose String Band, which played regularly over the radio at Columbia, Mis-

souri, in the early 1930s. His brother Dave also was a good fiddler, and both were characterized to me by Tony Gilmore as being "tough as shoe leather" in a fiddlers contest.

Uncle Joe Morrow spent most of his life in Texas until moving to Denver, Colorado, to live with a daughter. He recorded several tunes for me in 1949, including some in a category of old-time fiddle music which he described as "slow drags." He indicated that slow drags were popular years ago in east central Texas. I found this music fascinating, but I did not hear any of these tunes played at the annual convention of the Texas Fiddlers Association in 1950.

"Stick" Osborn of St. Joseph, Missouri, was recommended to me by Casey Jones, who called "Stick" a good fiddler. "Stick" was no longer playing regularly at the time he recorded for me in the early 1950s. He was among the many fiddlers who converged on Jefferson City for the state contests and playoffs in the 1920s. "Stick" operated a tavern at the time of my visit, but was maintaining the old Friday-night fiddlers-night custom. On Fridays he unplugged the TV, juke box, and pinball machines and made the tavern available to musicians who gathered for a long evening of old-time playing.

Charley Pettis of Anselmo, Custer County, Nebraska, was, for me, a genuine surprise. Here was an accomplished fiddler, living two hundred miles west of the nearest other Nebraska fiddlers of any repute (Bob Walters and Ed Mahoney), and in an area devoid of old-time square dances, with no accompanists in the surrounding locality. He had a substantial repertory of tunes for the ballroom in addition to a plentiful supply of traditional square-dance tunes. Charley mentioned on one occasion that an older brother had played the fiddle, and both were local natives. I am still puzzled by the isolated existence of this music in a location where, as far as I could ever ascertain, there was no historical tradition of old-time fiddling or dancing. Charley was playing for an occasional cowboy dance up in the Sandhills, but he told me those dance programs were all couple dances with a few waltzes.

Uncle William Raines, who lived in Morgan County, Missouri, near the Lake of the Ozarks, was perhaps the epitome of the old-time fiddler from rural Missouri. He was a farmer with several sons, all of whom were good jig dancers and callers. I once asked Uncle William at a recording session how many tunes he knew, and Uncle William answered by saying that he could "play all night," meaning, of course, that he would not have to play the same tune twice. Uncle William was the subject of an article in the *St. Louis Globe-Democrat*, which described his career, including his first-place win at the National Folk Festival in the late 1940s.

Aubrey Smith of Arlington, Virginia, is an old-time fiddler originally from West Virginia. He played on the circuit as a member of H. M. Barnes's Blue Ridge Ramblers in the Virginia–West Virginia area as well as on various radio stations in the 1920s and 1930s. At one time he was offered a recording contract by the Gennett Record Company at Richmond, Indiana.

Floyd Smith, who lived in rural Cole County, Missouri, was an office worker for the state during the day and a fiddler at night. He was a promising member of the new crop of Missouri fiddlers before an untimely death in the late 1950s. He recorded a group of tunes for me and invited the state champion guitar player to sit in on one of the sessions.

Dallas Stamper was operating the telephone exchange in Brumley, Miller County, Missouri, in 1926 when he was hired to fiddle for a six-day picnic and square dance at Dixon, Missouri, by Pat Scott, a local barber. I was hired to second on the piano for a dollar per night. Few fiddlers have ever impressed me as did Dallas Stamper, and I would be most gratified to possess Dallas's repertory and playing technique. Unfortunately, I can now recall only a small portion of the music Dallas played. He passed away in 1944.

Cyril Stinnett of Graham, Nodaway County, Missouri, attended the 1951 fiddlers' get-together at Frame Davis's in Des Moines. Cyril plays left-handed but had no trouble on the higher registers. His repertory included numerous tunes played by Bob Walters, but he did not play many tunes common to the Missouri Ozarks at this particular gathering.

Bill Stroll was a portly but distinguished elderly gentleman who attended the Walter Family reunion in 1951. I obtained no background information about Mr. Stroll except that he lived across the Missouri River, in Iowa. He played several tunes at the reunion and announced many tunes as Bob Walters played them at the gathering.

Robert E. (Uncle Bob) Walters was, by far, the smoothest fiddler I ever heard and knew the largest number of tunes of different kinds. It seemed extraordinary to me that Nebraska, a state where fiddling was so thinly distributed, would contain a fiddler of such high caliber. He was born in Decatur, Burt County, Nebraska, on the Missouri River. He was the son of Willis Walters who, reportedly, was a very good fiddler, and he was the grandson of

Ike Walters, a legendary fiddler in his own right, according to limited discussions with long-time local residents in Burt County. The Walters family emigrated from Kentucky to Iowa in the mid-1800s and eventually settled in Nebraska. Uncle Bob began playing as a small boy and complying with his mother's rule that he stand with his dad's fiddle extended over the bed to prevent dropping it on the floor. Uncle Bob was on the Sioux City, Iowa, radio on several occasions. He was forced to leave the farm because of poor health, and during part of World War II he had a radio program at Lincoln, Nebraska. He was playing over the radio at Grand Island, Nebraska, in 1949, when we began a series of recording sessions (on wire) which extended into 1958 (on tape). In addition to tunes learned through the family, he had picked up tunes from the radio, the old Edison wax cylinders, and from commercial records. His father had taught himself to read music and some tunes in the Walterses' repertory apparently came from such sources as *Gems of the Ballroom* (E. T. Root and Sons, Chicago) and *Beauties of the Ballroom* (John Church & Co., Cincinnati). We held twenty-nine recording sessions spread over ten years, and at each session Uncle Bob would invariably play one or more tunes I had never heard. I rank Bob Walters above all other fiddlers in ability to obtain pure tones and chords. He had an unusual method of tuning a fiddle by plucking and testing each string individually, never tuning two strings in unison under the bow. He reasoned that the only way to hear the true reaction of the violin to individual string tensions (and pitch) was to listen to a freely vibrating string, and that simultaneous vibrations on two strings, produced either by plucking or bowing, would obscure the points at which the violin body would produce its optimum response for either or both strings. He passed away in 1960.

Gus Vandergriff, a barber at Waynesville, Pulaski County, Missouri, in the 1930s was a competent fiddler, and the dances where Gus was playing were always enjoyable. I recall only a limited number of tunes Gus played.

Red Williams of Dallas, Texas, was stationed at the Lincoln, Nebraska, Air Base in World War II. He built a reputation around Lincoln as a good fiddler, and I visited him in Dallas in 1950. Red assembled the group he usually played with and recorded a large amount of Texas fiddling. After studying the recordings made at the Texas Fiddlers Convention that same year, I believe Red could take care of himself at a fiddler's contest anywhere in Texas.

Breakdowns

GRANNY, WILL YOUR DOG BITE?

This version is dissimilar to a tune of the same title in Ira Ford's book. On the other hand, Ford's "Tip Toe, Pretty Betty Martin" is similar to the tune given here.
Recorded by Bob Walters in November, 1949, and on several later occasions.

[2]

LAZY KATE

This version is comparable with "Lazy Kate" as published in Adam's book, where it is described as a typical Ozark mountain tune of about 1840.
Recorded by Bob Walters in September, 1950.

[3]

FRISKY JIM

Walters recalled that his father brought this tune home about 1905. No other fiddler has ever played this tune in my presence.
Recorded by Bob Walters in November, 1949.

[4]

LADY ON THE GREEN

This tune is a replica of "Hell on the Wabash," published in 1862 by Firth and Pond in a drummers' and fifers' tune book.
Recorded by Bob Walters in October, 1950.

[5]

Wake up Susan

Other titles often heard are "Up Jumped Susie," "Hop up Susan," etc. "Wake up Susan" is a two-part tune and is in most of the older collections. Howe, in 1864, published "Mountain Dew," a different tune, also in the key of A but having four parts. I have heard various mixtures of these two tunes over the years. The first two strains of Vee Latty's version are fairly close to the original "Wake up Susan." The first part of "Picnic Romp" in Ira Ford matches the first part of "Wake up Susan."
Recorded by Vee Latty.

[6]

Brilliancy

I have never heard a non-Texas fiddler play this tune.
Recorded by Red Williams in 1952.

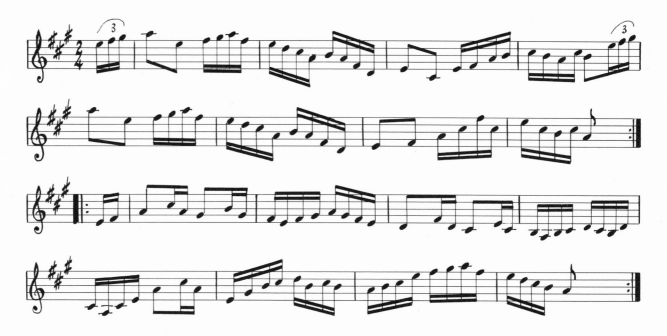

[7]

THE SCOLDING WIFE

I made little or no systematic effort to probe Uncle Bob for information on when, where, or from whom certain individual tunes came, including this one. I never heard it before nor since and can find no tune in the older publications which has the characteristics of being the source of this tune. Apparently this tune is traditional. Recorded by Bob Walters in April, 1954.

[8]

SALLY IN THE GARDEN, ASSISTING SAM

I have been unable to locate any piece in the printed collections that would appear to have been the origin of this tune.
Recorded by Uncle William Raines.

[9]

BEAR CREEK HOP

Recorded by Junior Daugherty in El Paso in May, 1949, prior to a fiddlers contest.

[10]

THE CAT CAME BACK

Played by a few Missouri fiddlers in
the depression days of the early 1930s,
but it is seldom heard any more.

[11]

LITTLE WHITE LIES

Recorded by Casey Jones in June, 1951.

[12]

JACK DANIELSON'S REEL

Recorded by Bob Walters at the first
recording session, November 20, 1949.

[13]

PARODY

This title was offered by Bill Stroll of Missouri Valley, Iowa, while Bob Walters was recording it in September, 1950. Mr. Stroll stated this tune was often used by fiddlers as a substitute when requested to play "Devil's Dream."

[14]

COMING DOWN FROM DENVER

Founded on "Lardner's Reel," which was published as early as 1864 by Howe in Boston. The first part parallels "Lardner's Reel," but the second part shows some modification. Recorded January, 1950, by Bob Walters, who was using it during his radio appearances over KMMJ, Grand Island, Nebraska.

[15]

GRAY EAGLE

This version contains some additions to "Gray Eagle" (in two parts) such as was published in 1935 in *100 WLS Barn Dance Favorites* (Chicago). "Gray Eagle" was also published in the key of B♭ in Harding's *All-Around Collection of Jigs and Reels* (New York, 1905). The tune in Ford's book (page 45), under title of "The Forked Deer," is a reasonable facsimile of "Gray Eagle."

Recorded by Floyd Smith in September, 1952.

[16]

JOHNNY, BRING THE
JUG AROUND THE HILL

Recorded by Bob Walters in January,
1950.

[17]
DOWN HOME RAG

Played by Tom and Eva, who had a morning program over KFEQ, St. Joe, Missouri, around 1932. Tom fiddled and Eva played a pump organ, and their music was enjoyable. This version is somewhat at variance with "Down Home Rag" published in *Original Dance Calls* by Will Rossiter (Chicago, 1926). An earlier commercial recording titled "Hell Among the Yearlings" by Herman Brothers (Broadway label #8165) is actually "Down Home Rag."

[18]

Money Musk

I have heard only a few fiddlers attempt this tune. Howe published "Money Musk" in two parts in 1864. An augmented version with four strains was published in the March 20, 1926, issue of *Dearborn Independent* by Henry Ford.

Recorded by Bob Walters in April, 1954.

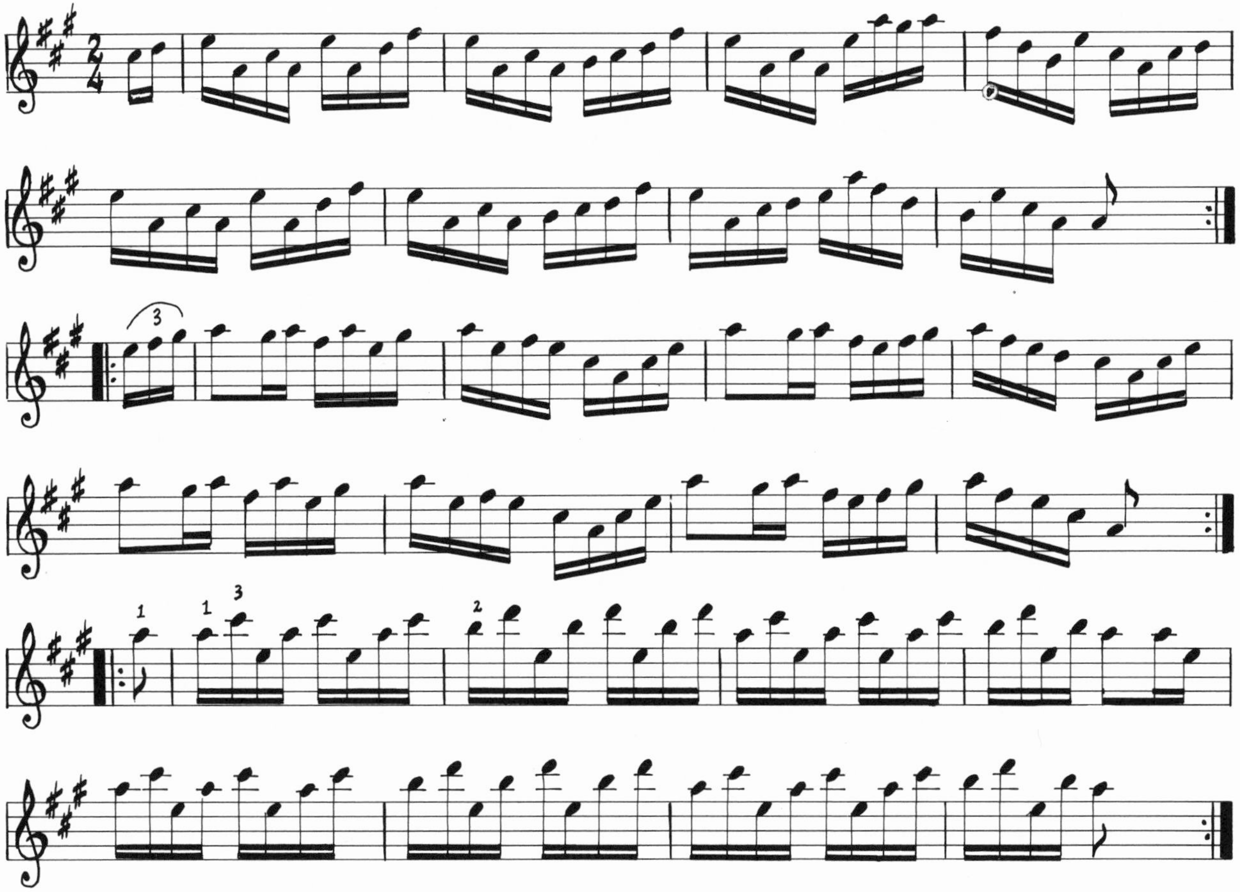

[19]

Boys Around the World

There are similarities between this tune and Bill Driver's "Sally Lost Her Slipper."
Recorded by Bob Walters in April, 1950.

[20]

Red Bird Reel

I requested this tune for comparison with a version being played at the time by a live band over KFNF at Shenandoah, Iowa. It is included here as part of the record, but there are other tunes more desirable.
Recorded by Bob Walters in April, 1950.

[21]

THE UNFORTUNATE
DOG

Title given here is a polite substitution
for use in mixed company. The correct
title is unprintable. Ford solved the
problem by calling his version "Rye
Straw." The three parts of this tune
purportedly depict a constipated canine
(1) suffering in labor following the
unwise ingestion of too many rye
straws; (2) howling in agony prior to
relief; and (3) yelping while leaving
the scene after the ordeal.
Recorded on wire by Bob Walters in
September, 1950.

[22]
PURCELL'S REEL

Recorded by Bob Walters in September, 1950. See note to #7.

[23]
DUNCAN'S REEL

This tune belongs with numerous others which I heard for the first and only time by Bob Walters. A "Duncan's Reel" was published by Howe, but it is an entirely different tune.
Recorded by Bob Walters in July, 1956.

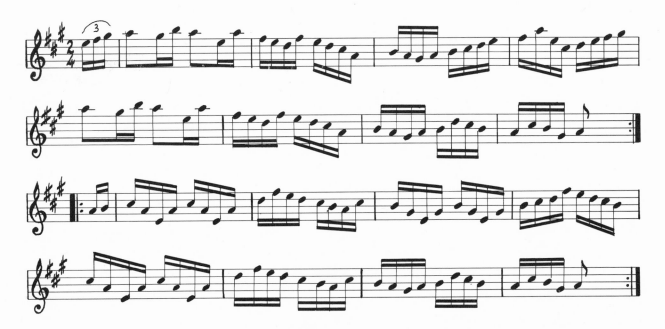

[24]

SLEEPY JOE

Walters played this tune with ease, even though it covers much of the fingerboard and requires some playing in the fourth position.
Recorded by Bob Walters in June, 1961.

[25]

GREEN MOUNTAIN HORNPIPE

Recorded by Bill Driver in August, 1950.

[26]

SALLY LOST
HER SLIPPER

Bill Driver played this tune at dances
and it was played also by many other
Missouri fiddlers, including Dallas
Stamper and my uncle.
Recorded by Bill Driver in 1948.

[27]

COTTON EYED JOE

This version is near most versions of
"Cotton Eyed Joe." Tradition around
my home town is that "Cotton Eyed
Joe" required special tuning of the
fiddle and was a good square-dance
tune. This version meets neither
criterion.

[28]

SALT RIVER REEL

Played by Casey Jones at Des Moines
in June, 1951.

[29]

PADDY ON
THE TURNPIKE

This tune has also been called "Jenny
on the Railroad." It is rather commonly
known among fiddlers and has been
in various tune books since Howe
published it in 1864 in the key of B♭.
Recorded by Bob Walters in January,
1952.

[30]
LAST NIGHT
IN LEADVILLE

This tune is a fair version of "Old Joe Sife's Reel," published by Howe. Recorded by Bob Walters in August, 1957.

[31]
THE DUSTY MILLER

Only a few of the many fiddlers I have known could play this tune. The version here is fairly close to "The Dusty Miller" that was played live occasionally over WSM, Nashville, Tennessee, years ago. One of the Howe books contains a tune of the same title, with a footnote that it is from a collection of Scottish music published in 1709. Howe's tune is 6/4 tempo, in the key of G, and bears no resemblance to the tune given here.

Recorded by Bob Walters in April, 1950.

[32]

PACIFIC SLOPE

Known in the Midwest, as Bob Walters played it regularly, and a guest fiddler played it in 1952 on KFNF radio, Shenandoah, Iowa.
Recorded by Cyril Stinnet in June, 1951.

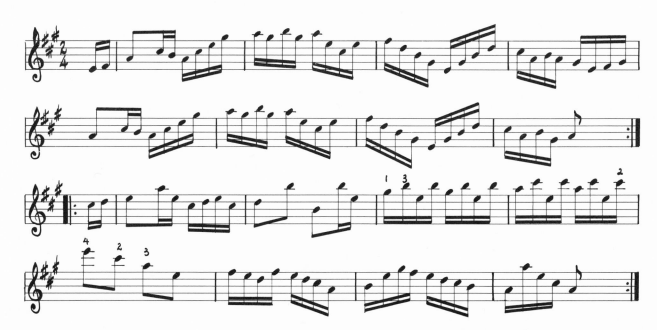

[33]

TOM AND JERRY

This version shows that only limited changes have occurred since 1864, when Howe published "Tom and Jerry."
Recorded by Ardell Christopher in October, 1951.

BILL CHEATUM

I did not hear this tune in Missouri
prior to the mid-1940s. Presumably,
this tune came out of the South.
Recorded by Floyd Smith in
September, 1952.

[35]
Breakdown

Bill Driver never did have a name for this tune, and it was identified locally as "the nigger tune." The first part is undoubtedly taken from "Lardner's Reel" (Howe, *Musician's Omnibus,* p. 52), while the second part seems to be wholly evolved from tradition. Another tune having the same characteristic structure, that is, the first part from "Lardner's Reel," second part something else, is found on an old 78-rpm recording, Okeh #45205, under title "Kansas City Reel." Recorded by Bill Driver, who played it often at the dance floor.

26

BREAKDOWN

Recorded by Bob Walters at a Walters
Family reunion in September, 1950,
when he played many tunes in succession and seldom announced any of
them.

[37]
BREAKDOWN

Bill Driver did not know the name of
this tune. The first part is taken from
"Kitty O'Neill," a jig published by
Howe and appearing in most books
of jigs and reels since then. The second
part is of unknown origin. The first
part of "Kitty O'Neill" is also the first
part of "Jack of Diamonds," a tune
played by some fiddlers in West Texas.

[38]
BREAKDOWN

Bill Driver used this tune frequently
at dances.

[39]
BREAKDOWN

Designated by Vee Latty as "Old Joe Clark" when he recorded it for me. In view of the characteristics of Bill Caton's tunes and the interpretation Bill gave to "Beaux of Oak Hill," I believe this is one of Caton's tunes, even though Latty played it.

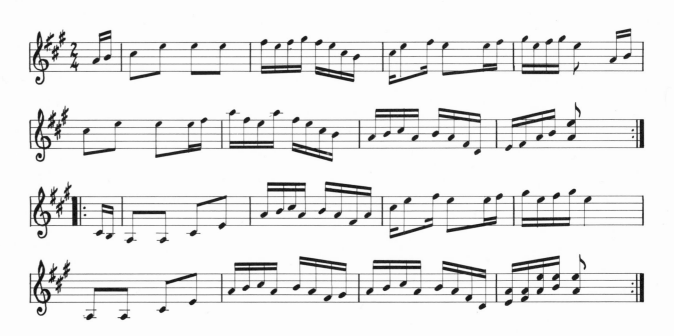

29

[40]
BREAKDOWN

By Bob Walters. It appears to be a
modification of "Ball and Pin Hornpipe," with an added third part.

[41]

BREAKDOWN

Uncle Bob Walters got this tune from
a Canadian radio program. It resembles
a tune called "Angus Campbell."
Recorded by Bob Walters in March,
1952.

[42]
High Level Hornpipe

Derived from "Highland Hornpipe,"
as published for years in various books
of jigs and reels. The original printed
version is rather difficult for many
fiddlers.
Recorded by Bob Walters in June,
1956.

[43]
THE SPOTTED PONY

Played by Tony Gilmore, about 1953,
this tune is attributed to Lyman Enloe,
a fiddler and onetime resident of Miller
County, Missouri.

[44]
LEDDY'S HORNPIPE

"Leddy" could be the name of some
fiddler, since this tune, in much its
present form, was published years
earlier as "Democratic Rage Hornpipe."
Recorded by Bob Walters in January,
1950.

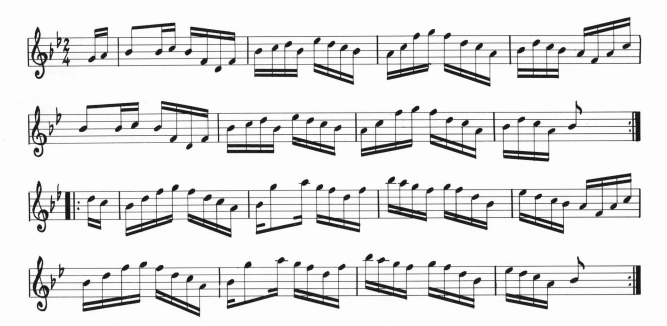

[45]

St. Joe Hornpipe

Recorded by Bob Walters in November, 1949.

[46]

Thunderbolt Hornpipe

Requires bowing skill of a high order for correct playing. The use of two 32nd notes to be played within the time allowed for one 16th note is indicated in the older printed collections. This technique is not heard today either live or on records, new or old, and Uncle Bob is the last fiddler in my acquaintance who had this capability. Recorded by Bob Walters in November, 1949.

[47]
EFFIE'S HORNPIPE

Original by me; it carries my pet name for my wife, Joan.

[48]
LONNIE'S HORNPIPE

Recorded in September, 1950, by Bob Walters, who mentioned he learned this tune from Lonnie Robertson, a fine Missouri fiddler who played over KFAB, Omaha, in the early 1940s with Bob Walters.

Key change notation is not traditional in fiddle music. It has been added here and elsewhere so the music will be easier to play.

[49]
CASEY'S HORNPIPE

Recorded by Bob Walters in September, 1950.

[50]

OLD MELINDA

Recorded by Bob Walters in November, 1949.

38

[51]

WAGNER'S HORNPIPE

"Wagner's Hornpipe" bears a faint resemblance to "Wagner" (or "Tennessee Wagoneer"), a well-known fiddle tune.

Recorded by Red Williams, who stated it is of local Texas origin.

[52]
Old Joe

Recorded by Bob Walters in May, 1951.

[53]
Wagner

Played by all fiddlers who recorded for me. It was published by Adam, Ford, and Routh, and traces back to "Belle of Claremont Hornpipe" in the older publications. Version given here is a composite: first part is mine, second part is Tony Gilmore's.

[54]
BILLY IN THE LOW GROUND

Also known as "Billy in the Low Land." It can be traced to "Braes of Auchentyre" reel in *1000 Fiddle Tunes* and to "Beaus of Albany" reel in Howe. Howe and *1000* have different titles for at least eleven other tunes. There are at least twenty in *1000* which have two or more titles. Recorded by Bill Driver in July, 1950.

[55]
JUMP FINGERS

Walters got the title and the tune years earlier from George Pounds, a fiddler in Burt County, Nebraska. Recorded by Bob Walters in November, 1949.

[56]

BREAKDOWN

This is one of Dallas Stamper's tunes. Recorded by Burnis Harrison, July, 1950.

[57]

BREAKDOWN

Bob Walters's father played this tune but did not have a name for it. Recorded by Bob Walters in December, 1956.

BREAKDOWN

Recorded by Bill Driver in July, 1950.

[59]
BREAKDOWN

Played by Dallas Stamper in 1926 at a picnic in Dixon, Missouri. I never heard this tune again until about 1957, when a fiddler in Indiana played a similar version at a square dance. In 1968 I visited this fiddler, who reportedly had learned it years ago, minus any name, from an old fiddler living along the Wabash River.

[60]

BREAKDOWN

I was advised by Mr. Cliff Clark, a
retired banker at Iberia, Missouri, that
this tune has been known in Miller
County for many, many years.
Recorded by Bill Driver in July, 1950.

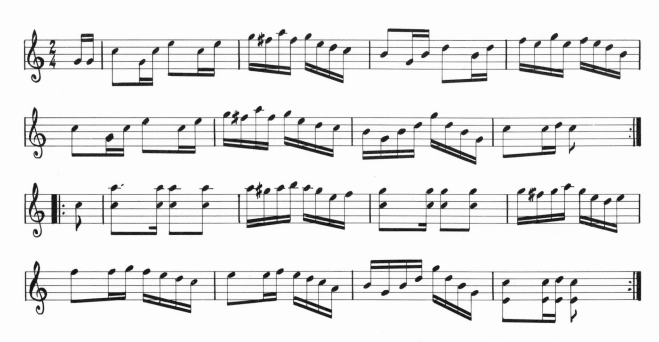

[61]

BREAKDOWN

Played by Fred Doxstadder. He identified it as "the opera piece."

BREAKDOWN

This breakdown in C is by Bill Driver.

[63]

THE LOST INDIAN

For years I have requested individual fiddlers to play "The Lost Indian." I have never heard the same tune twice, which might indicate that several Indians got lost. Adam, Ford, and Thede each published a different "Lost Indian." The version given here is merely to add to the list, and is not offered as the authentic tune. It would be most difficult to identify and validate any tune as being the original "Lost Indian." Various modern fiddlers will play "The Lonesome Indian" (as taken from a commercial recording of the early 1950s) when requested to play "The Lost Indian." A tune, "Step to the Music Johnny" in Ford's book, is similar to this version.
Played by Zeke Holdren.

[64]

BREAKDOWN

Recorded by Bill Driver in 1950.

[65]

BREAKDOWN

Recorded by Bill Driver in July, 1956.

[66]

BREAKDOWN

Walters's recollection was of learning
this tune in Minnesota where he had
gone to work in the small-grain harvest
one summer.

Recorded by Bob Walters in December,
1956.

[67]

TUNE

Played by an unknown fiddler at a
jam session at Onawa, Iowa, in late
1956.

[68]

MARMADUKE'S HORNPIPE

This tune is among the best for old-time square dances, and few, if any, fiddlers could play it as well as Bill Driver. Local fiddlers in central Missouri have mentioned this tune was propagated by Daniel Boone Jones, a widely remembered fiddler from Boone County, who represented Missouri in one of Henry Ford's national contests in the late 1920s.
Recorded by Bill Driver on December 13, 1950.

[69]

BUCK REEL

Recorded by Bob Walters in August, 1958.

[70]
LANTERN IN THE
DITCH

Recorded by Bob Walters in November, 1959.

53

[71]

BLACK EYED SUSAN

Recorded by Bob Walters in April,
1950.

[72]

HUNTER'S HORNPIPE

Derived from "Huntsman's Hornpipe,"
published by Howe in 1864.
Recorded by George Morris in August,
1953.

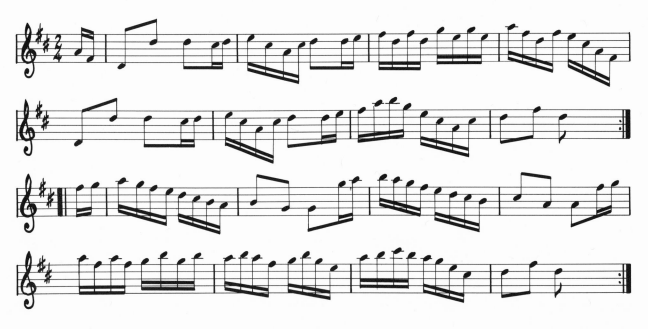

[73]
WOODCHOPPER'S
HORNPIPE

Played by Bob Walters at a square
dance in Douglas County, Nebraska,
in 1953. This tune was also heard at
the 1966 Old Fiddlers Convention
in Chester County, Pennsylvania, in
practically the same format.

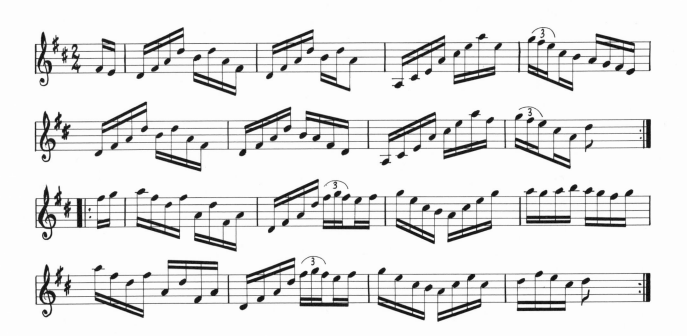

[74]

OPERA REEL

Played by Uncle Jimmy Lewis. It has been published in tune books for many years; the printed version is musically preferable to the way many fiddlers play it.

56

[75]

FISHER'S HORNPIPE

The printed version, in old tune books such as *Musician's Omnibus,* is written in the key of F and is more awkward to play. I recall two particular commercial recordings of "Fisher's Hornpipe" from earlier years. One was by Clayton McMitchem, who played it in four different keys in sequence. The other was by Georgia Slim, who played it in F but revised the second part of the tune and added a third part of his own. The accompaniment for "Fisher's Hornpipe" is demanding, if done properly. E. F. Adam published a fine piano accompaniment in his original book. Reprints of Adam's book by both subsequent copyright owners omit the piano accompaniment to all of Adam's tunes.

Played by Bob Walters in January, 1950.

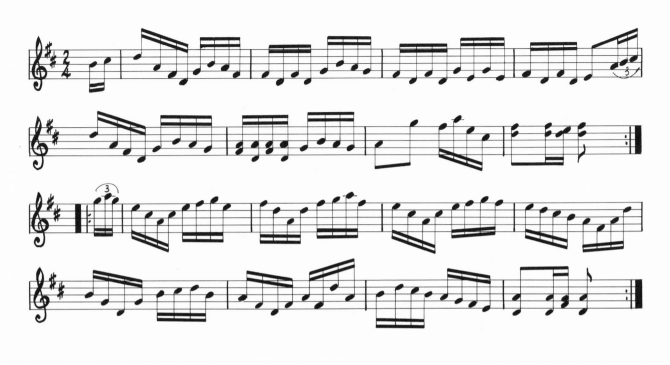

[76]

THE MISSOURI MUD

The second tune Bob Walters played during the initial recording session, November 11, 1949.

57

[77]

MONEY AND CORN

Played by most fiddlers around Dixon, Missouri; the version here is Bill Driver's. This is one of the less desirable tunes, with no great merit. It appears to be a descendant of "Wind That Shakes the Barley."

[78]

IRISH HORNPIPE

As announced by Bob Walters when he recorded it in January, 1950.

[79]
SMITH'S REEL

A comparison with "Smith's Reel" published in *Musician's Omnibus* by Howe (1864) shows the evolution that occurred in this tune as it was passed from fiddler to fiddler.
Recorded by Bob Walters, September, 1955.

[80]
OYSTER GIRL

Recorded by Bob Walters on Thanksgiving Day, 1951.

59

[81]
FIVE MILES
OUT OF TOWN

This tune has some resemblance to
"Old Dubuque."
Recorded by Frame Davis, September
24, 1950.

[82]
AUNT MARY'S
HORNPIPE

As played by Vee Latty. I never heard
this tune outside the Little Dixie area
of Missouri.

[83]
LIBERTY

The only Missouri fiddler who ever played this tune for me was Jack Croy of Morgan County, Missouri. One 78-rpm fiddle record titled "Liberty" was issued several years ago, but the tune was entirely different.
Played by Jack Harris in 1950.

[84]
OLD VIRGINIA REEL

As announced and played by Thomas Michaels. I consider this as one of the truly fine old-time fiddle tunes, and Mr. Michaels is the only person I ever heard play it.

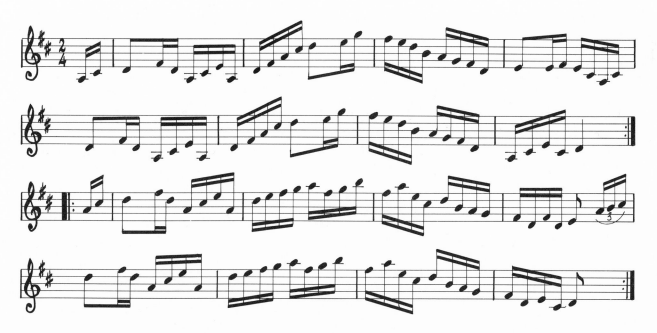

[85]
Two Bits

As played by Bob Walters, who credited it to Oscar Doty, a retiree in Missouri Valley, Iowa. Mr. Doty had a high-priced violin he had acquired from a member of the Omaha Symphony, and he played it in 1951 at the annual get-together for fiddlers sponsored by Mr. Frame Davis in Des Moines, Iowa.

[86]
Johnny, Don't Come Home Drunk

Recorded by Bob Walters, December 28, 1956.

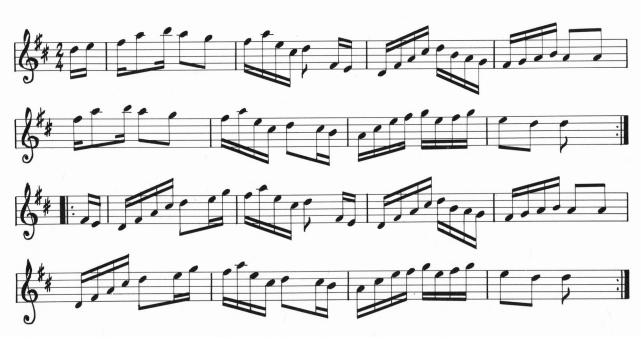

[87]

DURANG'S HORNPIPE

One of the better tunes for old-time
dances. It is in the key of D and is
structured so the fiddler can, if he
chooses, utilize an adjacent string as a
drone in parallel with the melodic line.
Playing on double strings will frequently enhance a tune and produce
more volume. In April, 1950, Bob
Walters played the tune approximately
as it was published in many of the
older tune books. Most other fiddlers
who recorded for me played it in the
modified or traditional style. The
version given here is close to the
version Bill Driver recorded in December, 1950. Ford published a very
good version. Adam lists "Wobble
Gears" as an alternate title for
"Durang's Hornpipe."

[88]

MISSISSIPPI SAWYER

Bill Driver's version. Red Williams of
Dallas, Texas, expressed an opinion
that "Mississippi Sawyer" is descended
from "Downfall of Paris," a tune
published at Boston by H. Prentiss in
the 1830s.

[89]

THE FORKED DEER

This tune bears considerable resemblance to "Rachel Rae," found in some of the older Scottish tune collections as well as in *White's Solo Banjoist* (Boston, 1896). Some fiddlers play the first part of this tune differently and use a portion of "The Forked Deer," as published in *Virginia Reels* by George Willig, Baltimore, in the 1840s. It is a version that is very perplexing for the accompanist to follow.
Recorded by George Helton, July 29, 1956.

[90]

JESSE CAIN'S TUNE

This title is for identification purposes only; it is not given as the correct one. Jesse never did announce it, and he was the only fiddler I ever heard play this tune. It is within the range of possibilities that Jesse improvised it himself.

[91]

Old Dubuque

This tune is known in northwest Missouri, having been included in a tune book written by Dr. W. H. Morris of St. Joseph, Missouri, in 1925. It is very similar to "Phiddling Phil" in Adam's book.

Recorded by Bob Walters, September 11, 1955.

[92]

Zack Wheat's Piece

As played by George Helton. This is another instance of a tune known only by the name of a man who played it. Zack Wheat was an earlier fiddler of some renown who lived near Argyle, Missouri.

[93]

Old Aunt Kate

Recorded by Bob Walters.

[94]

Rocky Mountain Goat

This tune was often used by the Helton Brothers in the 1920s for square dances at the annual Fourth of July picnics in Dixon, Missouri. Recorded by Ardell Christopher in October, 1951.

[95]
AMERICAN HORNPIPE

A seldom heard tune that appeared in the earlier printed collections.

[96]
HELL AMONG
THE YEARLINGS

Some fiddlers may play versions of this tune, obviously memorized from an early 78-rpm recording. The ending of the first part in the commercial recording is prolonged with extra notes, a disagreeable version for the accompanist. Ford's "Hell Among the Yearlings" (page 101) is a fair approximation of an old Missouri folk song, "Got a Little Home to Go To." Recorded by Bob Walters, July 29, 1958. A similar version was recorded by George Helton in July, 1956.

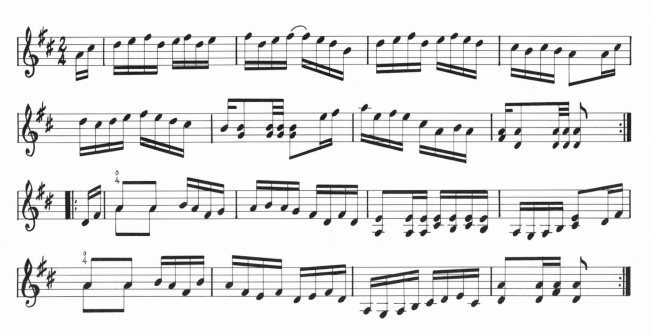

[97]

DRY AND DUSTY

As played by Gus Vandergriff. This tune was fairly common in central Missouri in the late 1920s and early 1930s. A commercial recording of "Dry and Dusty" appeared several years ago and was comparable in many respects with the version Gus played. A quite different tune under this title is in Thede's book.

[98]

BREAKDOWN

This tune is known by several titles. It was called "Richmond Polka" by Red Williams, who recorded it for me. The same title was used on a 78-rpm Brunswick record of about 1935 by Clark Kessinger. This tune is called "Redman's Reel" in Ford's book. A fiddler in Loudoun County, Virginia, advised me in 1962 that the title is "The Robert E. Lee Swing." Cy Kines has always known this tune as "The Rocky Road to Dublin."

[99]

BREAKDOWN

Tune by Bill Driver, who never had a
name for it. In several discussions he
attributed many tunes to his father,
who was a fiddling preacher in Laclede
County, Missouri.

[100]

BREAKDOWN

Played by Aubrey Smith for square
dances at Fort Belvoir, Virginia.

[101]

BREAKDOWN

Unnamed tune heard years ago over
the radio.

[102]

TUNE

By Bob Walters, who did not give
the title.

[103]

BREAKDOWN

Played by a performer at the Texas Fiddlers Convention at Athens, Texas, in 1950. A reporter from the *Fort Worth Star-Telegram* told me in 1965 that the annual Fiddlers Convention at Athens had long since been disbanded. Apparently there were increasing troubles with people who follow large gatherings.

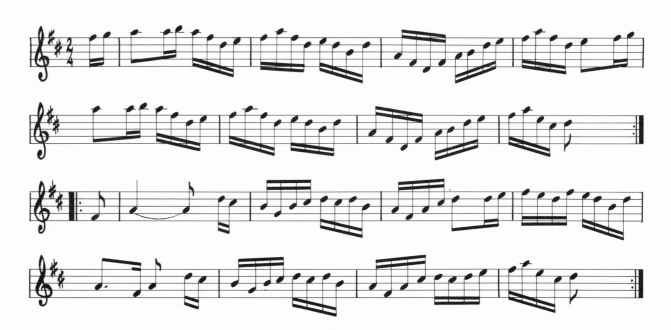

[104]

BREAKDOWN

Another tune played by Bob Walters without giving the title.

[105]

BREAKDOWN

Tune played by Bill Driver. My uncle
also played this tune, but I have never
heard it outside the Ozarks.

[106]

BREAKDOWN

Another tune by the Helton Brothers.

[107]

BREAKDOWN

Played but not announced by Bob
Walters. This tune, like others he
played, is not shown in previous
publications, and the original title
cannot be determined.

[108]

BREAKDOWN

Played by John Caton.

[109]

BREAKDOWN

A Bill Caton tune as played by Vee Latty. This tune is taken from "Beaux of Oak Hill," found in many of the old tune collections. "Lonesome Katy" in Ford's book (p. 57) is comparable with "Beaux of Oak Hill."

[110]

BREAKDOWN

Unnamed tune.

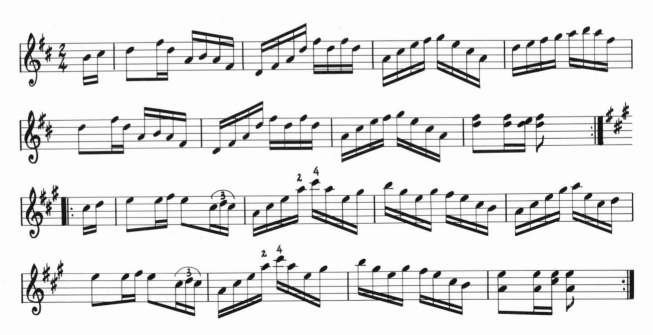

OH SAY OLD MAN,
CAN YOU PLAY
A FIDDLE?

Played by Red Williams.

THE DRUNKEN WAGONEER

This tune raises a problem in semantics: Is it "Wagner" or "Wagoneer"? Recorded by Bob Walters in April, 1950.

LADIES' FANCY

Recorded by Ardell Christopher in
October, 1951.

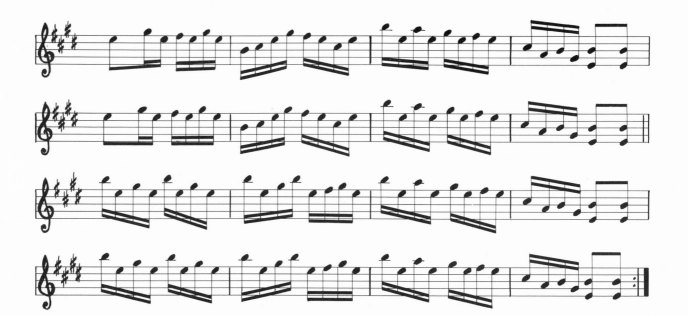

[114]

BREAKDOWN

Played by the Bell Family at dances in
New Mexico in the mid-1940s.

[115]

BREAKDOWN

Unnamed reel heard several years ago.

[116]

Constitution Hornpipe

The original version, as published in older tune books, is more difficult to play than this one.
Recorded by Bob Walters in December, 1951.

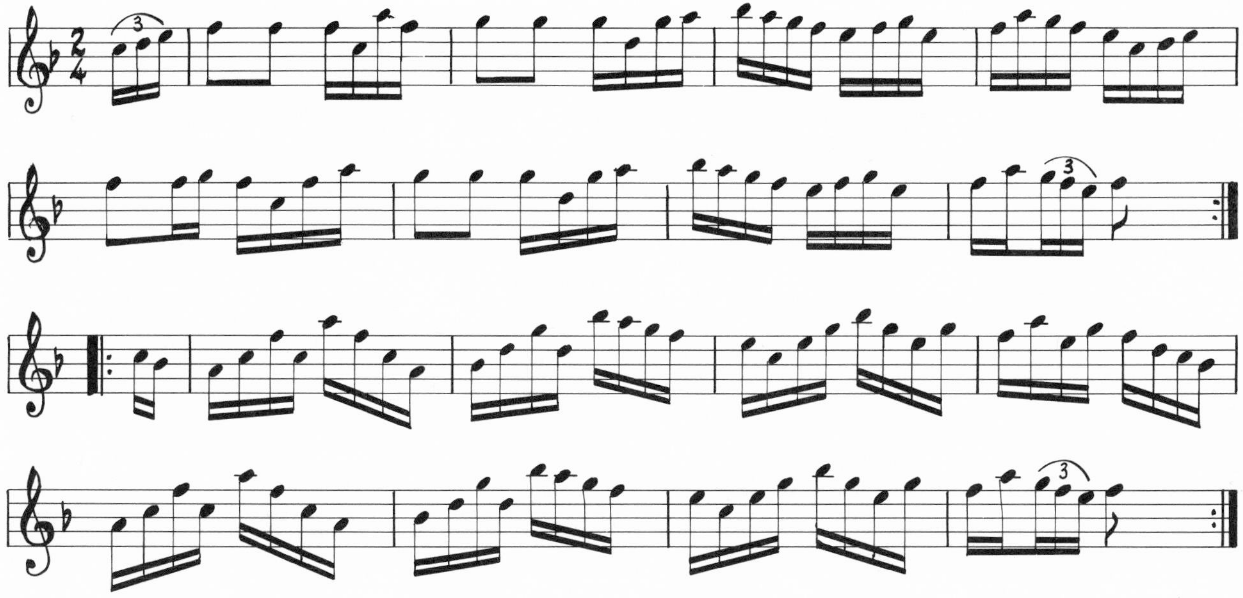

[117]

Breakdown

Recorded by Bob Walters in November, 1955.

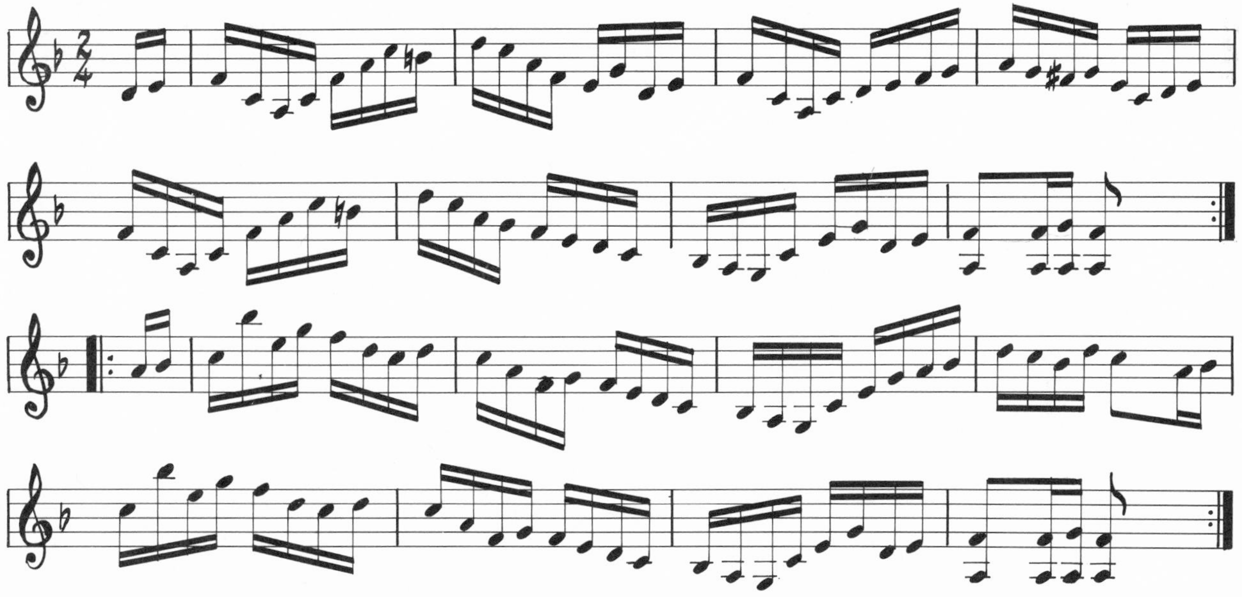

BREAKDOWN

Bill Driver often played this tune at
the dance floor during the annual
encampment at Iberia, Missouri.
Recorded by Bill Driver in July, 1950.

[119]

Jimmy in the Swamp

Recorded by Bob Walters in May, 1951.

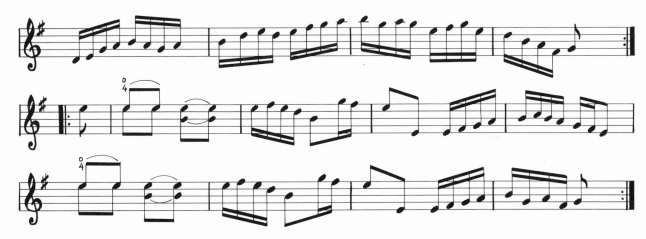

[120]

The Hollow Poplar

Recorded by Bob Walters in April, 1950.

[121]

ADRAIN'S HORNPIPE

Recorded by Bob Walters in November, 1949. I did not hear this tune again until 1968, when a fiddler on a live TV program in Missouri played it.

[122]

HOOKER'S HORNPIPE

Recorded by Bob Walters in 1949.

[123]

LEATHER BREECHES

As played by "Stick" Osborn. The basic movement in "Leather Breeches" is founded on "McDonald's Reel," which is carried in most books of jigs, reels, and hornpipes. The tune is usually played in three parts by most fiddlers, but extra embellishments are often heard and usually include a bowing effect parallel to the strings to imitate the sound of machine stitching.

88

[124]

BRICKYARD JOE

Played often by Tony Gilmore. Tunes of this type, in which the first two measures are repeated three times in succession, are fortunately rare.

[125]

CHICKEN AND DUMPLINGS

I have heard this tune only in the Southwest.

[126]

THE SHANGHAI ROOSTER

As far as I can ascertain, this is a
Midwest tune.

[127]

JORDAN IS A HARD ROAD TO TRAVEL

As played by Cy Kines. It is taken
from a minstrel song of the same title
written by Dan Emmett, composer of
"Dixie."

[128]

WALK ALONG JOHN

Mr. Tee Green of Phoenix, Arizona,
played "Walk Along John" at a contest in El Paso in 1949.
Recorded by Bill Driver in July, 1950.

[129]

RUN NIGGER RUN

A similar version is found in Ford.
A tune with 11 measures is found in
Thede's book under this title.
Recorded by Bill Driver.

[130]

BITTER CREEK

Apparently a local Texas tune, as I
never heard it before.
Played by Red Williams.

[131]

SALLY JOHNSON

Versions heard in other states are not always as elaborate as played by Texas fiddlers. Accompanists will often overlook use of the E-minor chord in "Sally Johnson." Various fiddlers have confusedly intermingled "Sally Johnson" with "Katy Hill."
Recorded by Jack Harris.

[132]
RABBIT IN THE GRASS

Played by Bill Driver.

[133]
LIMPING SAL

Another of Bill Driver's tunes.

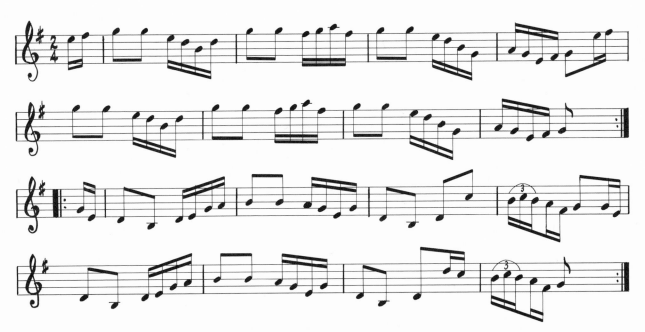

[134]

BLACK SALLY GOODIN

This is one of Bill Caton's tunes.
Played by Vee Latty.

[135]

Art Wooten's
Hornpipe

Recorded by Bob Walters, January,
1950.

[136]

THE IRISH COBBLER

This tune is now rarely heard, although fiddlers around Jefferson City, Missouri, including Tony Gilmore's nephew, played it earlier. Recorded by Bob Walters in November, 1951.

[137]
SCOTT NUMBER ONE

Bill Driver was the only fiddler who ever played this tune for me. Recorded by Bill Driver in September, 1950.

[138]
SCOTT NUMBER TWO

This tune was well known in Missouri. A version included in Ira Ford's book is under the title "Lane." Vee Latty often used the title "Fever in the South" when announcing this tune. Recorded by Bill Driver in September, 1950.

[139]

STONEY POINT

The last two of the four parts are
solely Bob Walters's. Most versions
consist of the first two parts, as shown
here. "Stoney Point" is descended from
"Kelton's Reel," published in *Ryan's
Jigs and Reels*. "Kelton's Reel" was
published as "Pig-Town Fling" in
*White's Unique Collection of Jigs and
Reels* (Boston, 1896). "Kelton's Reel"
has been recorded commercially under
the title "Wild Horse."
Recorded by Bob Walters in December,
1950.

[140]

KATY HILL

Recorded by Bob Walters, November, 1949.

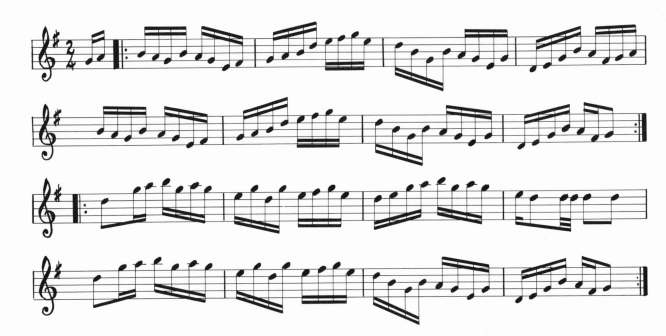

[141]

BULL RUN PICNIC

Identification was furnished by Cy Kines. A tune with much the same basic characteristics is published in Jarman's *Old-Time Fiddlin' Tunes* under the title "Williamsburg Reel." I draw no inferences from the fact that Mr. Kines is a Virginian and that Bull Run—the creek, and Williamsburg—the town, are also located in Virginia.

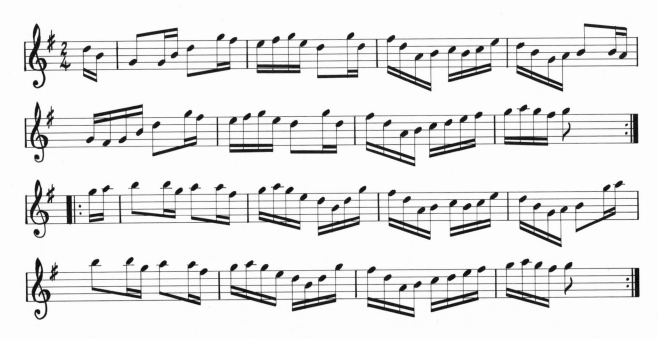

[142]

BLACKBERRY BLOSSOM

Comparable with the version commonly heard over the radio when the radio still had fiddlers. "Blackberry Blossom" in *1000 Fiddle Tunes* is an entirely different tune.
Recorded by Bob Walters in May, 1951.

[143]

THE OLD GRAY MARE

An adaptation from the well-known song. This tune is an exception to my lack of appreciation for songs, minus their words, being used as fiddle tunes.

[144]

SITTING BY
THE YELLOW GAL

A Bill Caton tune played by Vee Latty.

[145]

STEAMBOAT ROUND THE BEND

Recorded by Bob Walters, December, 1956.

[146]

FIDDLER'S DREAM

A fairly typical version.
Recorded by Bob Walters, September, 1950.

[147]

THE DARK HAIRED GIRL

Recorded by Bob Walters in August, 1957.

[148]

DANCED ALL NIGHT WITH A BOTTLE IN MY HAND

Not to be confused with "Give the Fiddler a Dram."
Recorded by Bob Walters in July, 1956.

THE OLD HEN CACKLE

As played by Tony Gilmore. There are
many versions of this tune, not all of
which are suitable for an old-time
square dance, as is Tony's version.

[150]

JOCKEY'S HORNPIPE

Uncle William Raines told me that
he heard this tune played so often
under or near the racetrack stands
at county fairgrounds in early days
that he called it "Jockey's Hornpipe."
True title is unknown.
Recorded by Uncle William Raines.

[151]

LONG JOHN

Recorded by Bob Walters, November,
1949.

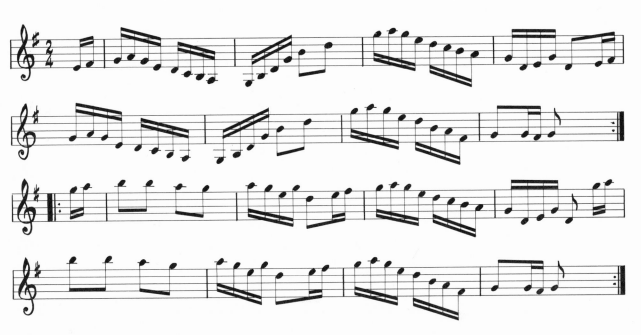

[152]

The Fox and Hounds

This tune is quite rare and is com-
pletely different from the traditional
harmonica solo by the same name.
Bluebird records issued "Fox and
Hounds" on #B-6753. To the tyro,
these tunes would sound quite similar;
for the experienced listener, they are
different.
Recorded by "Stick" Osborn in
February, 1954.

[153]

BREAKDOWN

"Wrecker's Daughter" is a title given to this tune by Joe Johnson, an ex-street entertainer, living in Lincoln, Nebraska, in the 1950s. He was an experienced guitarist for backing up fiddle tunes and presumably in a position to identify many tunes. This tune, however, is unlike "Wrecker's Daughter," published by Howe in 1861. It was known in my home town as "The Wild Goose Chase," but "Wild Goose Chase" was also the name of a popular square-dance figure for which this tune was most often played and its true title is unknown. Supertone Records (S-2089) once issued a "Wild Goose Chase" that was an entirely different melody.

[154]

BREAKDOWN

The second part of this tune bears a resemblance to the last portion of "The White Cockade."
Recorded by Bill Driver, July, 1950.

[155]

BREAKDOWN

This tune is another illustration of the metamorphosis in fiddle tunes. The parent tune is "Bummer's Reel," published by Howe in the 1860s. "Bummer's Reel" appears as "Levantine's Barrel" in *1000 Fiddle Tunes*. Recorded by Bob Walters, December, 1956.

[156]

BREAKDOWN

Played by Casey Jones at Des Moines, Iowa, in 1951.

[157]

BREAKDOWN

Played by Bill Driver. My Uncle Fred
also played this tune.

[158]

BREAKDOWN

Another Bill Caton tune.

[159]

BREAKDOWN

Another Bill Caton tune.

BREAKDOWN

Tune by Waldo Helton.

[161]

BREAKDOWN

Tune by Bill Caton.

[162]

BREAKDOWN

Unnamed tune recorded by Bob
Walters in August, 1957.
On this occasion, Uncle Bob recalled
hearing his grandfather play this tune
around 1900.

Quadrilles

[163]
ART WOOTEN'S
QUADRILLE

Recorded by Bob Walters in January,
1950.

[164]

STICKS AND STONES

Recorded by Charles Lutz.

[165]

DICK McGRALE'S JIG

A fairly obscure tune.

[166]

LITTLE RED WAGON

Recorded at Grand Island, Nebraska, on Thanksgiving Day, 1951, by Charles Larson, Bob Walters's cousin from Oregon who was visiting the Walters family at the time.

119

[167]

HASTE TO THE WEDDING

A well-known tune that appears in most of the older tune books.
The version here was recorded by Bob Walters.

[168]

OYSTER RIVER QUADRILLE

Recorded by Bob Walters in November, 1949.

[169]

MARCHING QUADRILLE

So designated by Bob Walters when he recorded it in September, 1955. According to the Walters family tradition, this tune was used in the Civil War. In my opinion, this tune is derived from "The Muckin' o' Geordie's Byre"; see *Allan's Ballroom Companion*. This tune is also one of the strains in "Grandpa's Favorite Quadrille," published in Henry Ford's *Good Morning* and credited to E. T. Root and Sons.

[170]

MISSION QUADRILLE

Recorded by Bob Walters, September, 1950.

[171]

A, E, & D Quadrille

This number is one of four parts of "Blue Bird Quadrille," published in Chicago in 1899 by E. T. Root. In the early publications the music for a quadrille usually consisted of at least three—more often four or five—numbers in different keys and tempos. Today's usage of *quadrille* commonly refers to a single number in 6/8 tempo. Recorded by Bob Walters in November, 1949.

[172]

QUADRILLE

Recorded by Bob Walters in December, 1950.

[173]

QUADRILLE

Recorded by Bob Walters's brother in
August, 1957.

[174]

QUADRILLE

Played by Bob Walters. He stated this
was the first tune he ever learned to
play.

[175]

QUADRILLE

Recorded by Charles Pettis in 1955.

[176]

QUADRILLE

Recorded by Bob Walters in November, 1951.

[177]

QUADRILLE

Recorded by Uncle William Raines.

[178]

QUADRILLE

Recorded by Bob Walters in November, 1955.

[179]

QUADRILLE

Recorded by Bob Walters in January, 1952.

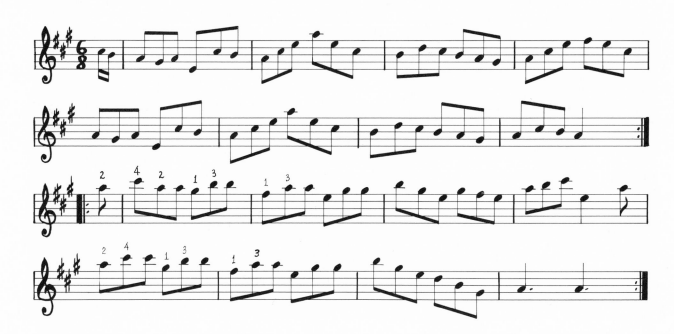

[180]

QUADRILLE

Recorded by Bob Walters in January, 1952.

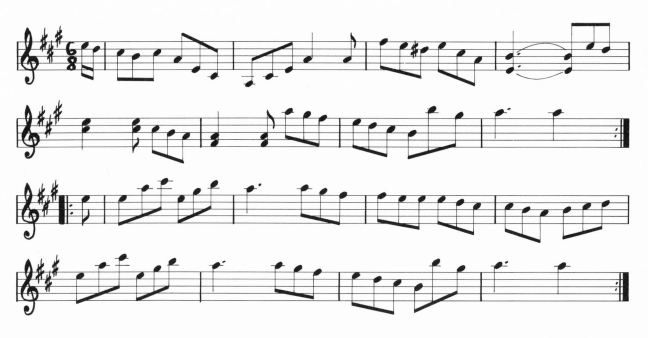

[181]

QUADRILLE

Recorded by Bill Stroll in September, 1950.

[182]

QUADRILLE

Recorded by Uncle Bob.

130

[183]

QUADRILLE

Recorded by Bill Stroll in September, 1950.

[184]

QUADRILLE

Does not conform to the historic pattern of music for the standard quadrilles. This music is suitable for a group of dancers who enjoy doing the two-step.

[185]

QUADRILLE

Recorded by Bob Walters in October,
1950.

[186]
QUADRILLE

Recorded by Bob Walters in November, 1955.

[187]
QUADRILLE

A faintly similar melody is found on a 78-rpm Harmony recording bearing the title, "Old Catville Quadrille." Recorded by Bob Walters in August, 1957.

[188]

QUADRILLE

Recorded by Bob Walters in January, 1952.

[189]

QUADRILLE

Recorded by Bob Walters in August, 1957.

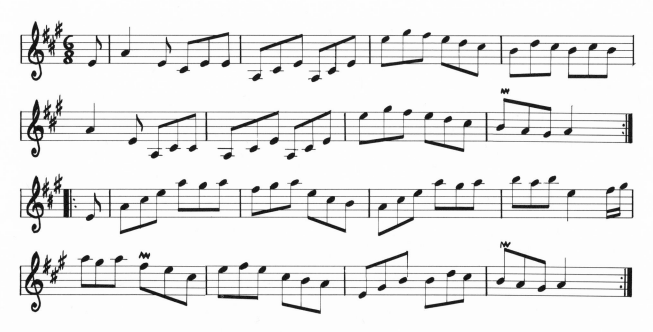

[190]

Quadrille

Recorded by Bob Walters.

136

[191]

QUADRILLE

Recorded by Bob Walters in November, 1951.

[192]

QUADRILLE

Recorded by Bob Walters in September, 1950.

[193]

QUADRILLE MEDLEY

Recorded by Bob Walters.

139

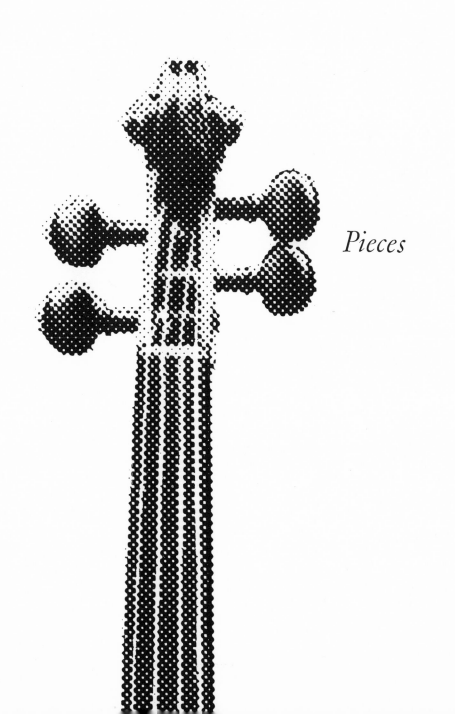

Pieces

[194]

CHARLEYTOWN
TWO-STEP

Taken from memory. I have never
heard this tune outside of Pulaski
County, Missouri.

142

[195]

OLD BALLROOM
TWO-STEP

It is highly probable this tune has
been published at some time in the
past, but I have been unable to find it.
Recorded by Bob Walters in August,
1957.

[196]

SILVER AND GOLD
TWO-STEP

Recorded by Bob Walters, who learned
it from a radio program years earlier.

[197]
JOHN BELDEN'S
TWO-STEP

John Belden was one of a trio of
fiddlers of considerable local fame who
lived in western Iowa years ago. The
other two were Frank Sexton and
Willis Kirkpatrick.
Recorded by Bob Walters in August,
1957.

[198]
QUICKSTEP #1

By Bill Driver.

[199]
QUICKSTEP #2

By Bill Driver. This tune could be
approximated by reversing the parts
in "Shaw's Reel" and modifying them
slightly.

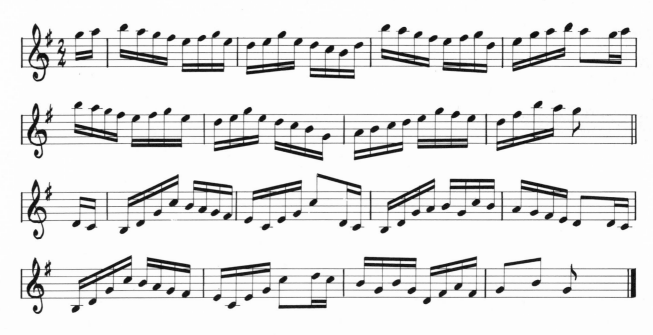

[200]

CRAPSHOOTER'S RAG

Recorded by Junior Daugherty in May, 1949.

[201]

BEAUMONT RAG

The fiddlers who played for me did not use the "Georgia lick," a bowing technique of fairly recent origin, which generates a syncopated accent. It is often used in "Beaumont Rag" and other tunes but can be quickly overdone, since it obscures the beat and throws accompanists off stride. It is one of the modern divertissements in present-day fiddling known as "hokum."

Recorded by Bill Driver and Red Williams.

[202]

TROMBONE RAG

Recorded by Bob Walters in April, 1950.

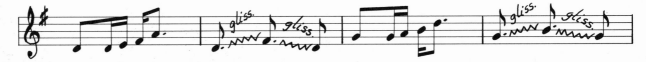

PEACOCK RAG

By Gus Vandergriff, who played it
frequently during 1934.

[204]

STONE'S RAG

Tune was known years earlier in
Missouri as "Whiskers."
Recorded by Bob Walters in September, 1950.

[205]

DIXON COUNTY BLUES

Recorded by Bob Walters in April,
1950. This is the only version I ever
heard.

154

[206]

JOE TURNER BLUES

This version is unlike the "Joe Turner
Blues" published in 1948 by Clayton F.
Summy Co., Chicago, which mentions
that Joe Turner was a policeman whose
job it was to take prisoners from the
Memphis jail to the penitentiary in
Nashville. W. C. Handy, famous blues
composer, wrote a song "Joe Turner
Blues," copyrighted in 1915.
Recorded by Red Williams.

155

KELLY SCHOTTISCHE

Recorded by Bob Walters in September, 1950.

[208]

SCHOTTISCHE

Played regularly at square dances in El Paso, Texas, in the 1940s.

[209]

TUNES FROM HOME

SCHOTTISCHE

Recorded by Bob Walters in December,
1950.

[210]

SCHOTTISCHE

Played at square dances by the Bell
Family.

[211]

SCHOTTISCHE

Played by "Blackie" Morgan at Fort
Belvoir square dances.

[212]

SCHOTTISCHE

Played by the Black Brothers at square
dances in Lake Valley, New Mexico.

[213]

BALTIMORE GLIDE

Recorded by Charles Pettis in July,
1955.

D.C.

[214]

VILLAGE POLKA

Played at dances at Fort Meade,
Maryland, by Cy Kines.

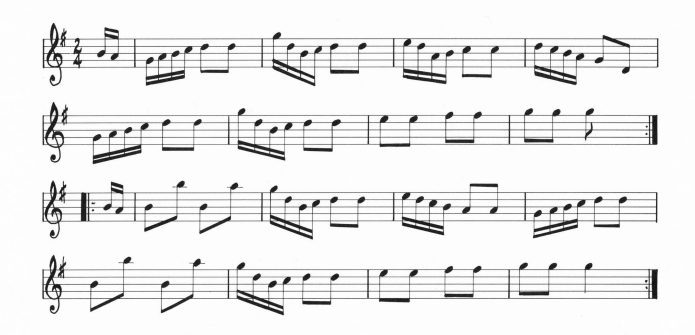

OLD PARNELL REEL

Recorded in January, 1950, by Bob Walters.

I have also heard the tune over radio WIBW, Topeka, Kansas, in the early 1950s when this station still used live talent.

[216]

OXFORD MINUET

The "Oxford Minuet," itself, was a regular item at dances in New Mexico-West Texas area, but the music was different and inferior to Uncle Bob's. Recorded by Bob Walters in June, 1956.

[217]

WAIT TILL YOU HEAR THIS ONE, BOY

I was never certain whether this was the true title or merely a statement Tony Gilmore would always make immediately prior to playing this piece. The correct title may be something entirely different, but no other fiddler ever played this piece for me. Recorded by Tony Gilmore in August, 1953.

[218]

RAGTIME ANNIE

Probably in the repertory of every fiddler. The version given here was recorded by Bill Driver and includes the third part in the key of G, which has been dropped by most modern fiddlers. Ira Ford omitted the G part.

[219]
Dragging the Bow

This piece became popular temporarily in the early 1940s after appearing on a commercial recording.
Recorded by Red Williams.

174

[220]

DONE GONE

A commercial recording was available in the 1930s, but has never been reissued. This tune is comparatively rare.

Recorded by Bob Walters in November, 1949.

ECHOES OF THE

OZARKS

This version is near the one given in
Ford's book. This piece has more
comparability with "The Yellow Rose
of Texas" as published in *100 WLS
Barn Dance Favorites* than with the
original version published in 1858.
Recorded by Bill Driver.

PIECE

"I Don't Love Nobody" was a coon song written by Lew Sully and published in 1896 by Haviland in New York. The melody in the chorus has become the common part in a cluster of two-part fiddle tunes whose differences are largely in the added part. "Crafton Blues," a Texas-based tune, is one; "Rock and Rye Rag" is another; "Walking Up Town" in Mom Routh's book is still another. A commercial 78-rpm recording of "I Don't Love Nobody" (Melotone #12746) follows this pattern and has a second part which I consider inferior to the first part. Various fiddlers, including Bob Walters, would play the Melotone version when "I Don't Love Nobody" was requested.

The version shown here was recorded by Bob Walters as an unnamed tune.

179

[223]
PIECE

Bill Driver called this tune a cake walk. I have met few modern fiddlers who could play a cake walk or three-step.
Recorded by Bill Driver in July, 1950.

CAKE WALK

This tune is derived from "Eli Green's
Cake Walk," published in 1896 by
Jos. W. Stern & Co. at New York.
Recorded by Bob Walters.

⊕ Coda

182

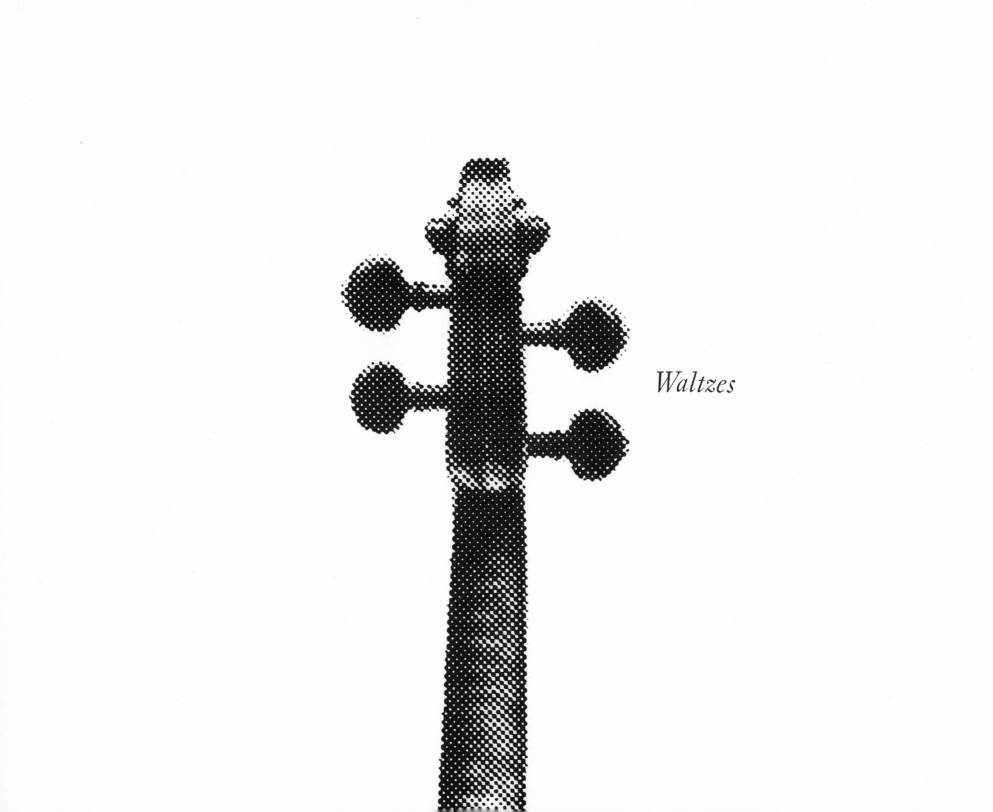

Waltzes

[225]

WALTZ

This waltz was often played by Waldo
Helton in the 1920s.
Bill Driver also recorded it in 1950.

[226]

WALTZ

Played by Dallas Stamper during a
visit to Pulaski County, Missouri,
in 1928.

[227]

STOP WALTZ

Recorded by Frame Davis in September, 1951. The same title has been used for other waltzes.

[228]

FRIENDSHIP WALTZ

My recording of this waltz was among a large part of my collection that was stolen out of storage in Missouri in 1966.

Recorded in the 1950s by Bob Walters.

[229]

S t e v e n ' s   W a l t z

Recorded by Bob Walters in November, 1949.

[230]

T h e   F o o t   T h a t

F a l t e r e d   W a l t z

Recorded by Bob Walters in April, 1954.

Joe Johnson's Waltz

This is a designation for identification
purposes. A brother of Joe Johnson
(see note to #153) would play the
fiddle during occasional visits to Joe's
home. Both claimed they jointly
composed most of this waltz, which
was lacking a satisfactory ending to
the second part. I worked out the
ending shown here.

ROSE WALTZ

Recorded by Bob Walters in December, 1950.

[233]

MORNING STAR WALTZ

Recorded by Bob Walters in August,
1957.

[234]

WALTZ

Recorded by Bob Walters.

[235]

WALTZ

Played by Bill Driver.

BUTTERFLY WALTZ

Played at the Texas Fiddlers' Association in 1950.

[237]

STARS AND STRIPES WALTZ

Taken from memory. It was often played over WOS at Jefferson City in the late 1920s.

193

[238]
TIPP'S WALTZ

Recorded by Bob Walters in December, 1951. It was played decades earlier by Willis Tippery, a barber in Burt County, Nebraska.

[239]

Played at a square dance in New
Mexico about 1948.

[240]

KELLER'S WALTZ

Commonly called "Kelly Waltz."
Authority for the title, "Keller's
Waltz," is Uncle Joe Morrow. He
claimed he knew Keller, who for a
time was a fiddler for a traveling
medicine wagon. According to Mr.
Morrow, Keller was in debt to a
saloon in Mangum, Oklahoma, and
offered to compose a waltz and play
it for the customers to settle the bill.
The saloonkeeper agreed, and this is
purportedly the waltz Keller composed.

197

[241]

GOODNIGHT WALTZ

Rather widely known. The version
here is by Bill Driver.

[242]
WEDNESDAY NIGHT
WALTZ

This waltz appears to have been founded on the song, "Wednesday Night Waltz." A copy was published in a Carson J. Robinson song collection in 1936.
Played by Red Williams.

[243]

SLEEPY WALTZ

Recorded by Fred Doxstadder in April, 1951.

[244]

SWEDISH WALTZ

Recorded by Bob Walters in January, 1950.

[245]
Waltz Quadrille

Played by Zeke Holdren as a medley he
apparently fitted together. This version
is very satisfactory for a set that wishes
to dance the waltz quadrille.

Accompaniments
for
Second Fiddle

Index of Tunes

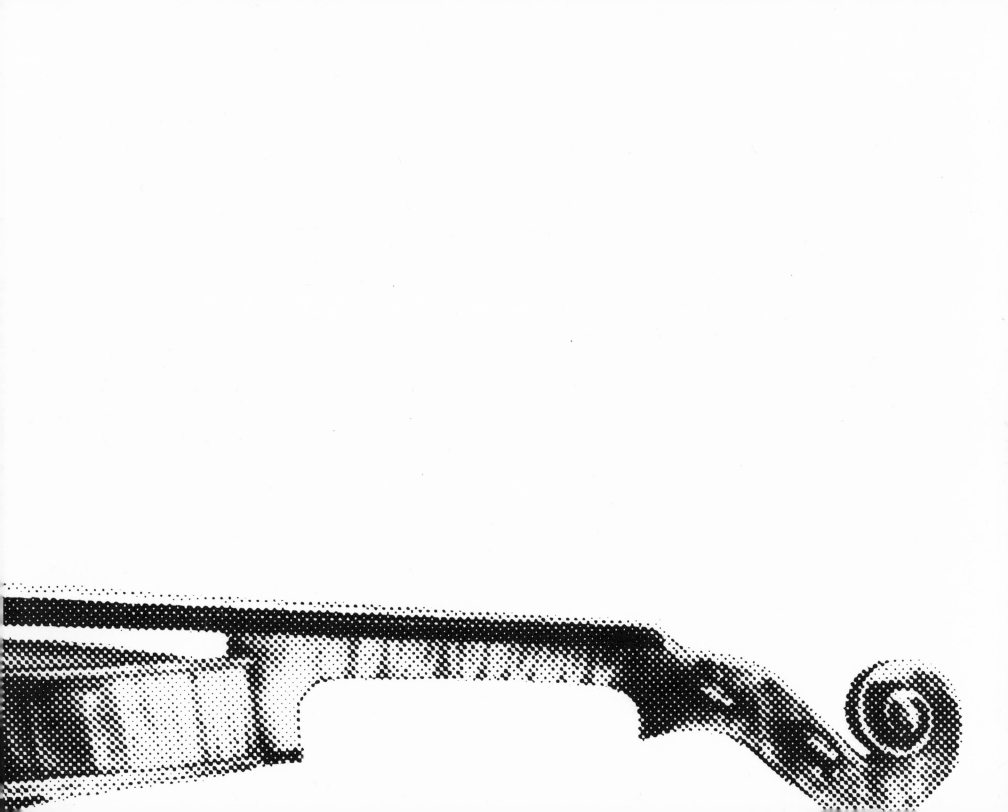

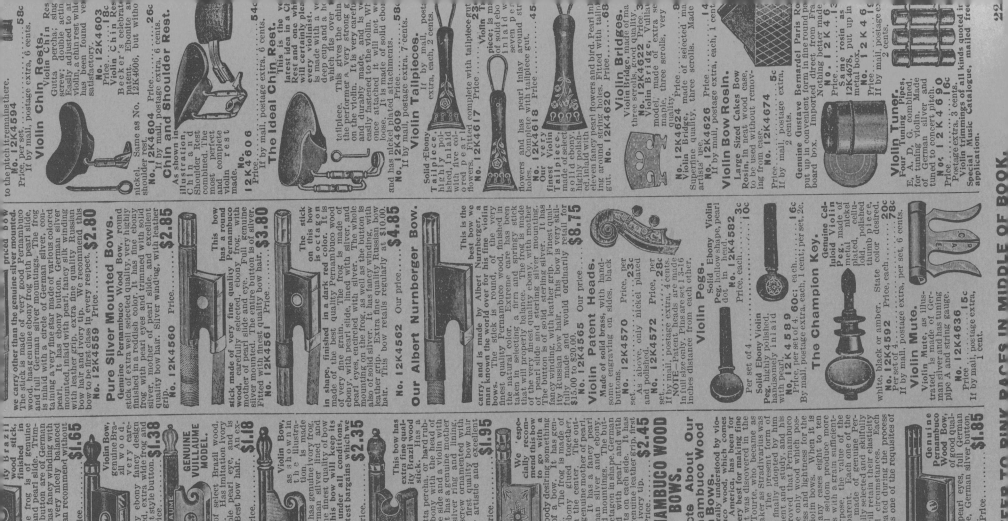
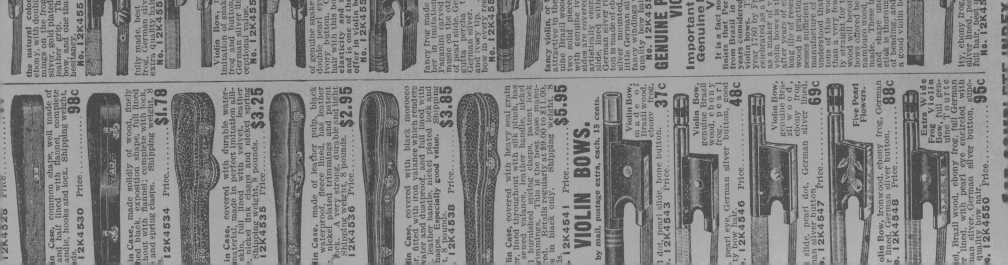